THE MONEY RESOLUTION

101 WAYS TO SAVE MONEY, MAKE MONEY & GET OUT OF DEBT IN ONE YEAR

BY FRANKIE CALKINS

ACKNOWLEDGMENTS

I wish to thank and acknowledge Claire Sander, Louis Sander, Alfonso Dueñas, & Rebekah Ray for their thoughtful help and support.

For mom, who taught me my first lesson in personal finance:
A penny saved is a penny earned.

ISBN: 9781795622950
Cover Design by Levina Robin.
Editing by Kimberly Gonzalez.

Disclaimer: The author may be compensated for linking to other sites or for sales of products this book links to.Although the author has made sure to include trusted links and websites, he bears no responsibility for any third party products, services, or websites. Author is not a Certified Financial Planner and this book is intended for entertainment purposes only.

www.TheMoneyResolution.com

CONTENTS

PREFACE

Money. That was my New Year's resolution one year ago. And as vague as that is, it was the only one I've ever stuck with.

When 2018 started, I knew (read: hoped) that I probably had a couple thousand dollars sitting somewhere in a dusty old 401(k) from a previous employer, but I had absolutely no idea how to track it down. When I had changed jobs, it became apparent that rolling the money to my new employer's plan was going to be a bit of a hassle, so I let myself forget about the money altogether. Classic millennial. The only reason I decided to even try to access it ten years later was to see if I could take the money out and put it towards my crippling student loan debt. Spoiler alert: don't ever do that.

Fast-forward a year. I read ten books; I followed ten podcasts; I watched tens (okay, hundreds) of hours of YouTube videos – all on the topic of personal finance. I tracked down all of my money. I invested it. I got a raise. I got a new job, which meant another raise. I got myself completely out of credit card debt, which was $15K at its worst. I opened two new credit cards and earned points: used some to travel, and saved the rest.

I improved my credit score by 25 points. I saved over $20K. I consolidated over $50K for retirement. I have an emergency fund and a rainy day fund. I have automated savings and investments. I'm on track to retire on time and hopefully early. Most importantly, I have goals, and I have a plan.

I did all of this while still being able to travel more than 40 days out of the year; I went to Europe for the first time ever! I accomplished all of these milestones and didn't have to starve myself or quit all my hobbies to do it. I didn't rob, steal, or cheat. I didn't even drive my girlfriend nuts (I don't think...). Oh, and I wrote a book!

Speaking of, this book and the above anecdotes are not meant to be a humble brag. For every success, I could tell you a story about a failure... including my foray with cryptocurrency. I'm not rich. Still quite the opposite, in fact. My net worth is actually still negative: I started at -$90K, but I've crawled back up to -$20K. (Plus, now I know what "net worth" means!)

Phew. That's out of the way. Still with me?

I'm not an expert, but I have learned a ton. This book will cover the specifics about what I did to accomplish the steps above, as well as provide many more tools and tips to help you in your personal finance journey. It will not cover owning property (not my wheelhouse yet) or tackling student loan debt, though some concepts will apply to the latter. Yes, buying a house is a goal of mine and yes, I will soon tackle my student loans head on and aggressively. But for me, I had to make a decision on how to prioritize my year of financial discovery: tackle my loans or tackle everything else? I decided on everything else. It's kind of like when you're dreading [insert overwhelming project here] so you decide to clean the entire house instead. I'm here to tell you how I did everything else in one year, and you can too! This book is about getting started, getting organized, and setting yourself up for long-term success and financial freedom.

A quick aside for context: I began tackling my personal finances through the very specific lens of a 30-something college-educated single male sharing an apartment in the heart of Seattle. You're probably not exactly like me. Modify the steps in this book accordingly to work best for your own needs and situation. If it makes sense to you, sort the steps or chapters to fit your own chronological path. Read it in any order after you read Chapter 1 if you'd like. Maybe you want to skip ahead to "Ten Things You Can Do Right Now". Or, maybe you're most interested in tackling the "Insurance" chapter right away. It's all up to you – there's no wrong way to read this book!

I wanted to share my story, warts and all, with full transparency because that's a theme that will come up multiple times in this book and is critical in successfully navigating your personal finances. You can avoid the doom and gloom all you want but it won't go away. Avoiding financial issues doesn't make you stuck, it makes you sink. I went weeks at a time for many years without looking at my bank account because I was terrified of what I'd see. This, my friends, is the first hurdle you absolutely must jump over: be transparent with yourself and, if you're in a financial partnership, be transparent with others.

Money is taboo. It's generally uncouth to ask a coworker what their salary is or to ask a neighbor how much they paid for their house. If we don't share this information with each other though, how do we know what's fair and how can we best advocate for ourselves? Talking openly about finances will only change when we start teaching financial literacy early on in schools, but that's best saved for an entire book itself... Unfortunately, this hush-hush mindset leads many people to approach their own finances secretively and without support.

If your situation was like mine, all you know is that you've dug a hole, so you avoid it altogether. We tell ourselves, *"how can I save when I'm living paycheck to paycheck?"* or *"what's the point? I'll never get out of debt."* You will. Maybe not immediately after reading one book, but this is a great first step. No more, "Yeah, but…" Take this time to open up your mind, believe in yourself, and try to adjust your thinking to "Yes, and…"

INTRODUCTION

"Success is the sum of small efforts, repeated day in and day out."
Robert Collie

I'm not one for cheesy quotes, but when I was a high-school teacher I had this one hung up in all of my classrooms. Once, before first period started, a student questioned it. He said, "Mr. C, does that mean I don't have to try *hard*?" I wasn't sure how to respond. *Well, yes and no...* I thought. Quickly I stammered, "It means, bring your best every day but don't get overwhelmed trying to be perfect. After all, showing up is half the battle." That's a lot of advice for a 9th grader to process before 9 am, but I saw the gears whirl inside his head. He nodded, flashed a thumbs-up, turned and settled into his desk. Later that hour, he volunteered to read aloud for the first time.

When I started college at the University of Washington in 2003, I set my mind to show up to class every day. Tired. Stressed. Hungover. It didn't matter. Just. Show. Up. It would have been easy to avoid some days. After all, the video of that lecture would be posted soon or I could just catch up over the weekend or somebody else probably took notes that I could borrow, plus I bet none of today's lesson will be on the final anyway...

So why go? Why show up every day? My motivation was easy because I had a goal: I wanted to be the first in my family to graduate college. Not only did I not want to fail, but I also didn't want to have any regrets: If only I would have gone to that extra study session. If only I would have bought the optional textbook. If only I would have Just. Shown. Up. (Yes, this story is a parallel to you and your finances!)

I don't have any regrets looking back at my college career. I don't regret switching majors or taking "Rocks for Jocks." I don't regret the debt that my degree put me in. But I do regret ignoring that debt, and then many others, for the decade that followed. Sure, I'd make small efforts here and there. But "here and there" was once a month, namely when I had to pay my bills and rent – *silent fist pump when the check cleared.* I wasn't saving any money, and my credit card debt was building. After college, I stopped showing up every day. That changed on January 1st, 2018, when I had had enough and finally decided "Today's the day."

Getting started was honestly the hardest part. Downright overwhelming after so many years of the "I'll deal with it someday" mentality. So I'll save you the trouble. This book is a real-life, up-to-date guide chronicling everything I did in just one year to get organized, save, and invest. I showed up every day: I committed to getting started, I persevered bumps, and I learned a ton that will help me for many years to come. So much in fact, that I felt compelled to share.

Many people think that getting your finances in order and learning what to do with your money takes years. People see phrases like "diversifying your portfolio" and "investing in a mutual fund" and assume those endeavors require appointments with an expensive financial planner. But it only takes baby steps, a little momentum, and a handful of quick and smart adjustments to get out of debt, save for now, and save for your future.

Use this book (and the included checklist) as your guide – try out 80 of these steps in the next year. Even if you completely fail at 30 of them, you can still boast FIFTY accomplishments in one year that improved your personal finances. That's four accomplishments a month. One *silent fist pump* every week. Even better, you'll be building positive habits that work for you for many years to come.

My intention is to cut the fluff by leaving out both the obvious (shop generic brands, skip a haircut, watch TV in *standard-definition* with an *antenna* – gasp!) and unrealistic (don't eat out ever again, recycle your toilet paper, join and win a fantasy football league) advice. This is not a cure-all but this is the comprehensive beginner's guide (with some intermediate and even advanced advice) you have been looking for. This book and its steps are meant to be accessible, relatable, and doable. Hopefully, most of the information you read is new to you and most of it is useful.

If I could do it on my own, you too can become financially intelligent in one year. You too can set goals, educate yourself, follow a plan (this one for starters!), and stick to it. Small efforts repeated day in and day out. My hope is that you quickly find that this is simpler than you thought and it spurs more interest in further financial education. This isn't a blueprint, it's a springboard.

Congratulations on this first step and good luck on your journey. Showing up is half the battle, and I'm glad you did. I can't wait for you to get started!

1
GETTING ORGANIZED

Sure, it sounds basic. Sure, it's probably not the sexy quick win you were looking for TODAY. But getting organized is easily the most important step you can take because this will set you up for long-term success. It's also a chapter I hope you come back to often because getting organized and changing life-long habits *will* take time. So let's jump right in and help you see your situation for what it is.

1 BE TRANSPARENT WITH YOURSELF.

Let's be real. It's time for you to understand the full picture. If you have debt, you need to understand how you got there because you can't fix the problem if you can't see what it is. It's time. Stop making excuses. Stop avoiding. Face any fears you might have. The best place to start? Let's get your financial documents and accounts organized.

My strategy to clean up the physical paper documents I had lying around (think tax forms, bills, notices from your bank, etc.) was to collect everything of importance into a little cardboard container from IKEA – you can get fancier if you'd like! –

and keep that box visible on a bookshelf. Weekly, I would open it up and see if there was something I could remove or organize further. My goal was to get the unruly pile of financial rubble strewn across my apartment into one organized and stream-lined system. This worked for me; you may prefer a desk orga-nizer or drawer system.

Digitally, I made sure I had logins for all of my accounts and bills. There were some I didn't even realize I *could* access online, like my Health Savings Account (HSA) and all those pesky old retirement accounts. Save the login information for these sites in one ultra-secure place (I recommend LastPass). While you're getting organized, log into all of these accounts at least weekly to get familiar and build a good habit of checking on them.

Getting organized both physically and digitally will help you see the full picture. It's that simple. I'm not asking you to start making changes yet, just take the baby step to sit down and really be transparent with yourself. But also… breathe. Remember, this is your year-long commitment.

2 REVIEW AN ENTIRE YEAR OF YOUR SPENDING.

Now is the time for a deep dive. Look at the last month of bank statements and find your top three financial offenders. Mine were shopping on Amazon, eating lunch out (#JimmyJohnsFor-Life), and overspending at the fancy boutique grocery store a block from work. Now, create a quick plan to reduce those expenses. Speaking for myself:

- First, remove my credit card information from Amazon.
- Second, commit to bringing my own lunch for one month.
- Third, just don't enter that fancy grocery store!

Every time I'm tempted to place a new Amazon order, I remember the eye-opening and horrifying moment after I had actually looked at my expenses and realized I casually racked up over $2,000 from shopping there in 2017. You might find that this step alone will help that voice in your head speak up in moments of financial weakness!

3 SET YOUR GOAL(S).

Figure out your "why" and work towards your "how" by determining the steps to get there. While there's tons of advice out there to help us goal-set, I stick to these three simple keywords: *challenging*, *measurable*, and *achievable*.

Here's a personal example of why and how I developed my goal to write this book:

- **Why:** I want to share everything I learned about personal finance so others might benefit.
- **How:** Organize all my notes in a way that sounds coherent and relatable. Share my personal finance journey somewhere, somehow... (YouTube? Blog? Book?)
- **GOAL:** Self-publish an eBook about my personal finance journey by January 31, 2019, so that others might be inspired to jumpstart their journey in 2019 and beyond.

Now it's your turn. Set your goals and, most importantly, stick to them! Remember: *challenging*, *measurable*, and *achievable*. If you're stuck, here are some examples (be bold and try 2 or 3!)

- Get completely out of credit card debt this year so I

can fully turn my attention towards investing and retirement.

- Open and max out a Roth IRA to start building tax-deferred compounding interest.
- Improve my credit score to 725 within 5 years so I can be successful in getting pre-approved for my first home.
- Save $5,000 for an emergency fund because life happens...
- Up my 401(k) contribution 1% each month until I hit 12% by year's end so that I can start building wealth that can grow towards my retirement.
- Try out 80 of the 101 tasks in this book because dammit, I'm determined to get my finances together in 365 days!

Enter your goal(s) on the official Money Resolution checklist at www.themoneyresolution.com.

4 TRACK YOUR ACCOUNTS AND SPENDING.

It's important that you're aware where your money lives and where it goes, otherwise, this is all a shot in the dark. I link all of my accounts through an online service called Betterment. Another favorite site of mine is Clarity Money: this rolls up your spending by categories and is less about amounts and budgeting. It can even help spot opportunities to save by pointing out that Netflix or Spotify subscription, for example.

Some people rave about Mint, and others love YNAB (You Need A Budget). To track spending, some might still prefer an old-school Excel spreadsheet budget, or even pen and paper! Check out all these methods and pick a way that works best for you. The most important thing is that your account balances and spending habits are transparent and accessible.

5 LINK ALL BILLS TO ONE CARD.

Here is one quick, tangible, and easy way to simplify your financial life *today*. I strongly suggest consolidating all of your bills to one card. Personally, I put all my daily expenses on one card and bills on another. Keeping my expenses consistent and simple allows me to spend more energy on the bigger financial goals, not worrying whether I have enough money spread over ten accounts to pay my bills. Make it simple for you to track your expenses, especially if you're doing it on your own. If you prefer to watch your cash in and cash out closely, use your debit card. If you're out of credit card debt and want to play the "points game", use your credit card (plenty more on this later).

6 CHANGE YOUR BILL DUE DATES.

Yes, you can do this! I recommend having as many due dates moved as possible to coincide with your pay schedule. For example, if you are paid on the 1st and 15th, reserve the first payday for housing and the other payday for bills. This helps to make your budget predictable and consistent throughout the month. There is no fee to change your bill due dates, but it generally takes an actual phone call to get it done.

7 TRACK DOWN OLD RETIREMENT ACCOUNTS AND CONSOLIDATE.

When I first started to access my retirement accounts, I didn't think I had more than a couple thousand in my past and current plans. After tracking them all down, getting organized, and upping my contribution, I ended up with roughly $50,000 between my IRAs and 401(k)s (all of it invested!). Roll over all those pesky company 401(k) accounts to one place, be it your current employer's plan if eligible or a personal IRA. It takes time, persistence, a sometimes annoying amount of paperwork, and especially patience. But it's absolutely worth it to have your money in one easy-to-access account that you can easily track, monitor, and tweak if necessary.

Here's a personal anecdote: I recently found a few thousand in a 403(b) from an old employer that had been making a measly 2% return for years (we'll learn more in a later chapter, but that's terrible). Rolling that money into my personal IRA, which gains 7% on average, was a huge financial boon. IMPORTANT: do NOT be tempted to cash out any of your retirement accounts. The tax implications, penalties, and fees are massive (think 20-25%+)!

8 DOCUMENT YOUR JOURNEY.

This is the fun part! You don't have to write a novel, just jot down any and all successes. This will keep you motivated and accountable. I created a basic "note" in my iPhone Notes app and entitled it "Accomplished in January" (and so on for each month) – easy! Start your story, and read it every once in a while for inspiration as you look back on your successes, small and large. For my advanced learners, add a "To Do This Month" or "Failures/Lessons Learned" section. Think parking tickets, late fees, splurges that you regret, etc. I even tracked unexpected expenses in the same note.

Organizing your notes by month allows you to reset and take a deep breath frequently throughout the year. There were also times that I opened Notes on the 25th of a month and realized I had only accomplished half of what I had the previous month. That was all the motivation I needed to get my butt back in gear and start tackling more in a hurry!

Here are other resources for documenting:

- Google Docs - Especially helpful if you're working on your finances with a partner.
- Trello - Great for visualizing tasks and moving things around by category.
- Excel - Keep track of hard and fast numbers in a good ol' fashioned spreadsheet.
- A reminders app - Most don't think to use it this way but it's great to help you quickly set a reminder to do something at a set time or place. Siri (Alexa, Cortona, Bixby...) can help you out on the spot! "Hey Siri, remind me to pay rent on Monday." "Hey Siri, remind me to pay for utilities when I get home." "Hey Siri, remind me to follow The Money Resolution on Instagram & Facebook in one hour." Reread that last part aloud just to be safe...

2

REDUCING EXPENSES

"Beware of little expenses, a small leak will sink a great ship."
  - Benjamin Franklin

We all have blind spots. Most of us struggle to truly understand the difference between needs and wants. The truth is, we all have money leaks we can plug. Combine that with the opportunity to think and plan ahead, and you'll be amazed at the amount small tweaks can make on your bottom line.

9 FIND AND ELIMINATE YOUR LATTE FACTOR.

Simple math: $5 latte a day, 5 days a week = $1,300 a year. Not to mention tax, tips, and that $3 warm buttered croissant you might be tempted to add...

Even if you don't drink coffee, chances are you splurge on something near daily. Many of us buy things as a reward for getting through our day. Some of us do it because we're creatures of habit and think we *need* to buy something to survive.

Track your purchases closely for a week to find your latte factor. Then try to go a week without it. Do the math and find out how much you saved... chances are, you'll be amazed by the amount! Plus, maybe you find there are TWO latte factors you didn't even know you had!

10 CANCEL THAT GYM MEMBERSHIP YOU DON'T NEED.

Here is an excellent example of needs versus wants. That fancy gym membership that you hardly use? That's not a need. There are countless ways to stay fit for free. Run outside. Explore local bike trails. Hike on the weekend. Play soccer in the park. Search on YouTube for ways you can do a total body workout in your living room in 30 minutes... all for free!

A word if you simply "can't even" with this one: at the very least, find the cheapest local gym in your area and hunt for special offers. Sometimes if you sign up with a friend or significant other, you'll get a better rate. Most gyms offer a free trial week so take advantage of this before committing. Be sure to ask if they will waive the registration fee – they want your business after all.

Personally, I followed my local gym's Facebook page after seeing a previous Facebook-only special offer. I patiently waited until I finally saw a Cyber Week special for new members. My point here is if you're one that needs to frequent a gym, try to find creative ways to lower this cost.

11 GET A COSTCO (OR SIMILAR) WAREHOUSE MEMBERSHIP.

It might seem counter-intuitive that I'm telling you to add a new annual bill, but sometimes you need to spend a little money to save a lot of money! You can split these annual ~$50 memberships with one other person. *Any* other person – a family member, a roommate, a friend, a neighbor, a co-worker, someone you find on Reddit!

Good purchases: toilet paper, paper towels, dog food, laundry detergent, toiletries, batteries, ibuprofen, breakfast bars, olive oil, nuts, most beer and wine, Brita filters, and meat (if you plan to freeze it).

Purchases to avoid: a new living room rug because "it's such a good deal", avocados (they will go bad before you eat all ten, I promise), electronics, gift cards bundles for movie theaters (unless you break up and gift them!), vacation packages, credit cards, and fancy beer and wine.

> **Frankie's Finer Points**: If you're not sure you want to join, ask a member for a Costco gift card. You can shop without signing up! You'll be able to compare how the essentials you stock up on stack up to your local stores or you can opt to use it on gas! You can also enter through the exit straight to the food court...

12 SLASH YOUR CELL PHONE BILL.

Chances are, you're paying too much for your phone. There are lots of methods for tackling this one:

- Join (or take the lead on organizing) a family plan. You can have multiple lines on one account but be sure you sign up for unlimited data, otherwise, that can be a hairball to monitor. The more people you have on the plan, the cheaper per person – oh, and it doesn't have to actually be "family". My brother mentioned to me he has seven people on his plan because of his wife's family and friends. Nice guy... but where's my invite?
- Another need vs want: skip the new model. Phones are designed to last more than 2 years!

- Dead set on buying the new model? Pay for it in full if you can. This can save you the headache and trapped feeling a contract brings and lighten up your monthly budgeting in the long term. When I recently purchased mine upfront, I was pleasantly surprised that my monthly bill came down $30 a month. Plus, now I'm keeping my eye out for a "ditch and switch" special at a competitor since I'm contract-free.

- Don't forget to sell your old phone. You'll get more value selling it yourself rather than trading it in.

- Protect your phone with a durable case. I suggest the Commuter Series OtterBox. It's okay to spend $20+ here, especially if you've decided to skip insurance (Spoiler: I recommend doing so in Chapter 11). If you do break your screen, be aware that replacing it via a third party will likely void your warranty and eliminate your opportunity to trade the phone back in.

- Depending on how your plan penalizes data overages, consider going for unlimited. Overages can really sneak up on you, especially if you like to stream videos or music on the go. You can look through your historical data usage in your online portal to see if this makes sense for you.

At the very least, don't leave your phone poolside in 100-degree heat for an hour while on vacation in Austin, Texas. I learned that baking your phone also voids your opportunity for a trade-in...

13 NEGOTIATE YOUR INTERNET (AND/OR CABLE) BILL.

If you've been with your internet and/or cable provider for less than a year, odds are you are on a special introductory rate. Call them before the year ends and ask them to honor the price for the next year. Threaten to cancel your account if needed – do some research online and have a specific competitor and "deal" in mind. Even if you've been with your provider for over a year, call them and see if they can't do anything to lower your bill. Nine times out of ten, your provider will not want to lose you as a customer and will work with you. If you have no luck, look at different plans and consider dropping your speed or reducing your channels to save money.

Frankie's Finer Points: Buy your own modem and router if you haven't already. I bought my modem router 2-in-1 for about $70 from Amazon while I was *at* Comcast signing up for my new account. Renting can cost you $120 *every year*! I do not recommend buying a second-hand router or modem. There's no guarantee that it will work and/or it may break shortly after you get it (this is one of those failure moments I mentioned that I'm skipping over in the interest of time and sounding smart!).

14 REDUCE THE BIGGEST BILL OF ALL: RENT.

Rent. The biggie. The truth is, you should always shop around when you're nearing the end of your lease. You simply never know what else is out there. You might find a better rate. At the very least, you'll be able to make an educated decision when you renew your lease. And when you do renew, *always negotiate.* The worst they can say is "no." Don't forget, finding good new tenants can be a hassle that many would rather avoid.

Look around your current place. Do you need all that square footage? Do you really need that breakfast nook or second bedroom that you never use? Do you need those high ceilings and "old world charm"? Or do you just *want* it? If you live alone, consider roommates. If you pay for parking or storage in your building, try going without next month and see if you actually miss it. Have the option to lock in a better rate if you commit to a two-year lease? Do it!

Frankie's Finer Points: Start your lease between November and February. I've been on this cycle for over 5 years. You'll have less competition which means, as homeowners and building managers get desperate, they will often give you a better rate! You have more control over the process and landlords would rather work with you than have to replace you in those bleak winter months. The most expensive time to look? June, July and especially August.

3

BANKING & SAVINGS ACCOUNTS

When I began my resolution to fix my finances, banking wasn't even on my radar. I had been a loyal customer to Bank of America for 15 years and assumed it would be a huge hassle to switch. I was able to look past all their downsides (fees, fees, and more fees) and focus on the positives, like how they have ATMs *everywhere* – even traveling! Once I took off my rose-colored glasses, I realized that there are much smarter options for my money – and yours!

15 SHOP AROUND FOR A NEW BANK.

Leave the big bank that charges you a fee just for having a debit card, or charges $12 for "general service". What does that even mean?? My suggestion? Look into a local credit union. Mine has *no service fees* and even covers up to $10 a month in accrued ATM fees when using any ATM. They're also extremely transparent about earned interest with a separate column next to my account balances. On my $3,000 average account balance, I've earned almost $20 this year in interest – free money just for storing my money!

Plus, local credit unions truly care about YOU. When it comes to loans, it helps to have an actual relationship with your bank. When you call, you'll get a friendly voice quickly (instead of waiting on hold for 30 minutes) that you may even recognize. Mine also never has a line to reach the teller window after filling out forms. You just sit down 1:1 at a desk to get help or use the indoor ATM. (plus, it's always warm and always safe)

A year ago, when I first joined my local credit union, I didn't realize they had a policy on only six withdrawals per month out of your savings account. I had withdrawn upwards of 10 times and accidentally racked up something close to $80 in transaction fees... 100% my fault. But I noticed it and when I called my credit union they reimbursed me in full. Super classy! The big banks wouldn't care to do that.

> **Frankie's Finer Points**: If you do decide to switch banks, ask about referral bonuses. Your significant other, friend, or family member can get $100 for signing up, and they'll push $100 your way too, for example. Just be sure you read the fine print: these kinds of offers tend to require a minimum balance for a set period of time (mine was $500 over 3 months).

16 CHECK YOUR BANK ACCOUNT OFTEN.

Don't ignore it. It can be scary, but the more you check your account balances, the less surprised you'll be. You'll notice when your account balances are low, when checks have cleared, or when a pesky "maintenance fee" shows up that your bank started. You might even find a fraudulent charge and be able to argue for a refund.

Once you're in the habit of looking at your money, set up auto alerts with your bank so you're always in the know. It's even easier to check your bank accounts on mobile, so be sure to download your bank's app.

I saw an interesting fact recently – only a little over 60% of Americans have at least one app on their phone related to finances[1]. While I'd like to assume the other 40% carry a laptop everywhere, I know that's not the case. That means over a third of the population is not taking a (literal) hands-on approach to their finances, and as we know – transparency with yourself is key! Put your bank's app on your home screen. Install your credit card's app. I created a folder in the bottom right (closest to my thumb!) with all the financial apps I use regularly. Here's a look at my folder:

Opt out of paper statements while you're at it. If anything, they're just confusing since you get the snail mail sometimes weeks after the activity in question has occurred. Don't forget, the internet is essentially real time!

Frankie's Finer Points: Set up text alerts when more than $100 is pulled out of your account. This has helped me catch mistakes and fix them immediately, avoiding any confusion or fees. You can even set up notifications for *any* transaction if you *really* love notifications!

17 OPEN AN ONLINE HIGH-INTEREST SAVINGS ACCOUNT.

Did you know that the rate of inflation in the U.S. hovers around 2%[2]? This means that if you kept all your money as cash under your bed, it'd actually be losing value every year – your $100 cash in 2017 would only net you $98 of goods in 2018. Today, the average savings account from a big bank will yield you between 0.01-0.08% APY (annual percentage yield - or interest). There's no way that rate can keep up with inflation – you're *losing money.*

Invest your savings in an online-only high-interest savings account. I highly recommend Ally. They currently boast 2.2% APY on all balance tiers with no minimum account balance. Plus, like traditional banking, they offer debit and credit cards and they also have excellent 24/7 customer service via a simple phone call or online chat. Compare, switch, ditch and save using websites like Magnify Money… that might be the actual slogan ingrained in my brain as a sponsor of my favorite podcast Stacking Benjamins.

18 GET YOURSELF A CD.

No, I'm not telling you to get out the old Walkman… I'm talking about a Certificate of Deposit (CD). A CD is a savings vehicle with a fixed maturity date and interest rate, between 2.65-3.63% APY for a good one[3]. Usually, CDs also have a minimum account balance. Essentially, you agree to park your money in a CD account for an agreed upon amount of time – anywhere from six months to ten years – and in return, you get a hefty rate of return compared to a traditional savings account.

CDs are excellent if you are saving a chunk of money for a future expense and you can't risk the volatility of the stock market (think: down-payment fund, vacation next year, etc.). CDs are not a good idea if you think you might need to dip into them – there are often fees associated if you terminate the agreement prematurely.

19 BUILD A SAFETY NET.

Did you know most Americans (61%) don't have enough money to cover a $1,000 emergency[4]? While $1,000 is an excellent place to start for beginners, aim to grow yourself a safety net big enough to cover at least three months worth of living expenses in case of an emergency. The key is to keep this money readily available because emergencies don't tend to hold themselves off for 3 to 5 business days.

Be prepared for just about anything life can (and inevitably will) throw at you – including layoffs, a family emergency, a pet emergency, a medical issue, a broken water heater, car issues, and so on. Make the contributions automatic so you're not tempted to skip your monthly contributions. I set up my emergency fund through Betterment: a super easy to use online ("robo") investment site. Others I know use Wealthfront, a similar platform, and love it.

Don't forget: if you have money put away for an emergency, USE IT for emergencies. One mistake I made in my past was telling myself to not *ever* touch the $3,000 I had sitting in savings, even when an emergency did come up. I went ten years letting this cash sit idle while I booked last minute emergency flights on my credit card (when already in debt).

Extra Credit: Try the Tip Yourself app.
Tip Yourself is a free app that lets you pay yourself. You can

do this for a variety of reasons. Many people tip themselves after completing chores like working out, cleaning the house, paying bills, taking the dog to the park, or grocery shopping. I give myself $5 for going to the gym and $2 more for a trip to the grocery store. There's a social aspect to it and gamification makes saving fun and easy. The money doesn't make interest so this shouldn't be your strategy for building wealth – instead, this is a fun way to keep yourself motivated as you work hard to accomplish your financial goals. If you find a similar app, make sure it's FDIC insured before moving any of your money into it.

CREDIT & CREDIT CARDS

According to the U.S. Federal Reserve, the average household in 2017 carried $137,063 in debt[5] . For people under 35, the number is more palatable at $67,400[6]... but yikes, that's still a *lot* of debt. For some, this chapter might be the first moment of feeling that tightness/sickness in your stomach – reducing your internet bill is nothing compared to staring at your debt head-on. Don't panic. I've outlined some easy strategies and tips below.

Once I climbed out of my credit card debt, I learned that credit cards can be fun! I had a blast researching cards with the best rewards and was shocked to learn about some of the crazy cool perks like covering the cost for getting TSA Precheck, fancy lounge access at airports, cash back, and sometimes free gifts!

20 SIGN UP FOR A FREE CREDIT REPORT.

Every person has a credit score – a number between 300 and 850 that essentially indicates to lenders how reliable you are with your money. A score of 700 or above is considered "good" and will gain you lower interest rates on loans and access to better credit card offers. Your credit score is constantly changing, and is largely influenced by these factors:

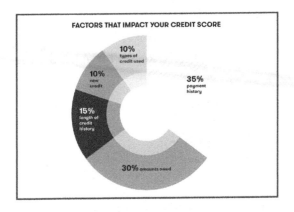

FACTORS THAT IMPACT YOUR CREDIT SCORE

10%
types of credit used

10%
new credit

35%
payment history

15%
length of credit history

30% amounts owed

Source: 5 Key Considerations for Improving Your Credit Score, The Points Guy[7]

Start by digging through your payment history to see if you have anything showing up as "not on time." Many people are able to find errors this way, and a simple phone call to your lender can instantly improve your credit score.

Another excellent way to stay on top of your credit is by opening a free Mint account; not only does Mint send you regular credit score updates, but you can also sync all your bank accounts in one place, track financial goals, create a budget, and so much more.

Set up email alerts when your score goes up or down. See a historical chart of your score. Learn more about the different categories that make up your score and how they are weighted. Find inquiries from the last two years that are still showing up on your report. And lots more! There are many easy, quick ways that you can improve your score – upping those points is almost like a game!

21 HAVE PAST FEES REMOVED.

Dig through your credit card statements. Do you see any late fees in the last year? Simply call the number on the back of your card and ask if they are willing to remove any of the charges. Feel free to remind them what a great and loyal cardholder you are! If this is your first time asking, they will usually do it – often times with no questions asked. Just don't make late fees a habit.

> **Frankie's Finer Points:** Set up auto payments. No excuses! You'll never get hit with a $25 late fee again.

22 NEGOTIATE YOUR INTEREST RATE DOWN.

Call your credit card company and negotiate your interest rate. Even just decreasing your rate from 12% to 11% APR (annual percentage rate) can really help if you have a high balance – that 1% on a $10,000 balance is a difference of $100 a year. Every little bit counts when you're crawling back to a zero balance.

You may not always be successful but it is always worth a try, especially if you've been a long-time card holder – most credit card companies would rather work with you to lower your interest rate than lose you to a competing company. And if they don't want to work with you… see step 23!

23 INITIATE A ROLLOVER ON A "NO INTEREST" OFFER.

NerdWallet has an article on the "Best Balance Transfer and 0% APR Cards of 2019"[8] – check it out! Rollover your high-interest debt to the "no interest" option if you have one or find a new offer. There might be a charge to do so but it can absolutely be worth the savings in interest, especially if you think you can pay all (or most) of the debt off during that no-interest introductory period.

24 PICK A PAYMENT STRATEGY AND STICK WITH IT.

The most popular methods these days for tackling debt are called the "snowball" and the "avalanche" strategies. The snowball strategy is to pay off your loan with the lowest balance first until you reach zero, while the avalanche method is to attack the loan with the highest interest rate first (both while still making minimum payments on others balances of course). The snowball method is a good way to boost morale, build momentum, and achieve mini-victories as you see your loans literally disappear, while the avalanche approach frankly makes the most financial sense and will reduce your debt faster.

Personally, I prefer and recommend the snowball method because it offers hope, and I believe success with money is more psychological than it is educational. I've come to realize personal finance is 80% attitude and behavior, and small victories usually lead to positive thinking and better habits. Either strategy is valid though, and it's up to you to decide which approach will keep you motivated. Try this handy Snowball Vs Avalanche Calculator from Magnify Money[9] to help you choose.

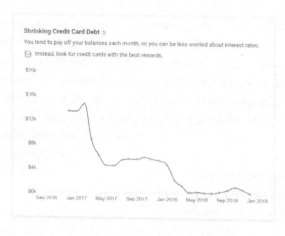

By picking a payment strategy and sticking with it, I was able to annihilate my credit card debt.

25 PLAY THE CREDIT CARD GAME

IF you are at a point where you are able to pay off your credit card balance each month in full, shop around for a new card with an awesome sign-up bonus and/or reward system that compliments your financial goals: 2% cash back, travel bonuses, redeemable points, retirement benefits, etc. Don't overthink the interest rate because you will be paying off the balance in full each month.

Here's what I picked (mostly travel-focused, as that's a priority for me) and others that I recommend for certain situations. But, as always, be sure to do your own research and make the right decision for you.

1. I recommend the three Chase cards I considered: Freedom, Sapphire Preferred, and Sapphire Reserve. Compare them at

NerdWallet here. My personal favorite is the Reserve card which currently offers a 50,000 point sign-up bonus when you spend $4,000 in the first three months. While this card carries a hefty $450 annual fee, $300 a year is automatically reimbursed on charges spent on transportation or travel. I spend this easily on Uber rides around town, parking, and airline tickets so for me it's essentially a $150 annual fee. It also comes with some incredible perks like Priority Pass for airport lounge access (more on this later), TSA Precheck or Global Entry reimbursement, rental car insurance, and more. If you're a big traveler, it can easily pay for itself.

2. My other favorite for travel is the Capital One Venture Card. This card currently has a lower $95 annual fee, waived in the first year. You earn 2 miles for every dollar you spend on every transaction, perfect for the person who doesn't want to think about purchase categories when picking a card. Plus, you can transfer miles to over a dozen airline partners and earn 10x points when booking through partner hotels. It also offers several of the same perks as the Sapphire Reserve card.

3. For you non-travelers, I know many people who swear by the Fidelity Rewards credit card. With this ~no annual fee~ credit card, you get unlimited 2% cash back on purchases across the board *if* you deposit the cash back into a qualifying Fidelity retirement account. Not the most immediately sexy card, but it's certainly a great way to boost your retirement contributions without having to think about it like, at all.

As with most tips in this book, *be patient with yourself* when dabbling with new credit cards. Don't be in a hurry. If you see a great sign-up deal, be sure to research and be extra sure that this is the card for you. Really dig into the pros and cons. The two sites I use the most to compare credit cards are The Points Guy and NerdWallet. Again, and I seriously cannot stress this point enough, ONLY play the rewards game IF you're in a position to pay off your credit card balance in full every month.

5

FRUGALITY

"Most of us value things more than we value money, which is why most of us have more things in our closets and cupboards than we do money in our bank accounts."- Suze Orman

Frugality is a hot topic these days (e.g. Mr. Money Mustache and r/Frugal), and it might be the toughest chapter to master if it's not a familiar concept for you. With that said, these tips aren't meant to turn your life upside down or strip you of all human basic needs and happiness. Don't give up the things you love to do just because you're being frugal – or you'll burn out and drive yourself crazy. You can be smart *and* save money with just a few easy lifestyle adjustments. Sure, individually, some of these steps may not feel worth it. BUT when you add them together you'll find huge savings in your bank account!

27 PLAN YOUR MEALS.

Sit down and think about what you want to eat for every meal this week. Now's the time to dust off your old Pinterest boards dedicated to fun recipes. Spending a little time upfront to plan will save you big bucks in the long haul. Then, make a list before you go to the grocery store and *stick to it!* Of course, take advantage of unexpected sales, but don't buy that full-price 10-pound tub of Nutella because it just looks so good.

I make my list in my default Notes app. My girlfriend likes to write hers down on a pad on our fridge and bring a pen. Another great resource for couples and roommates is the free version of the app AnyList – you can both add and delete items from the same list, so you can coordinate your shopping trips seamlessly and keep each other up to date when you're out of items. Try different methods and find what works for you!

> **Frankie's Finer Points:** Try out Ibotta, a rewards app that gives you cash back when you buy groceries. You just load deals onto your account and then take a picture of your receipt after you shop. Today I got back $2.50 on items that I was going to buy anyway. The free money adds up, my account has given me $166.12 in lifetime earnings to date!

28 BRING YOUR OWN LUNCH TO WORK EVERY DAY.

While this one might veer towards the obvious advice I promised to avoid, this part is the kicker: every day. Commit to it! Pack up your dinner leftovers. Stock up on inexpensive frozen microwaveable meals (for example, a filling butter chicken entree from Trader Joe's sets you back just over $3. Eating the same meal at a restaurant will cost you at least three times that). Do whatever it takes to B.Y.O.L. and avoid eating out! Don't worry about feeling judged; the truth is, by the end of the year you'll be judging the people you see coming back to the office with $15 takeout salads that they eat at their desk while they work... what schmucks!

Note: Don't penalize yourself if you're dragged to a work lunch with coworkers, just order responsibly.

29 TRY OUT A MEAL KIT SUBSCRIPTION SERVICE FOR DINNER.

Meal kits for dinner. You've heard of them all: Blue Apron, HelloFresh, Plated, Dinnerly, etc. Take advantage of their first-time customer sign-up bonuses, and try some out! Just make sure to set a calendar reminder to cancel once your trial is over.

The other day, I received an offer for $60 off my first three deliveries with one of these services – that ended up being three recipes for two people at a total of $33.94, or $5.66 per meal (including shipping!). Not only is that an amazingly good deal for a meal, but these services are fun and take the stress out of cooking (if you're not much of a chef, like me).

Keep your recipe cards so you have inspiration to remake your favorites in the future. Typically, you can even take advantage of the same sign-up offer by using an alternative email and delivery address. Send the kit to work if you have to!

30 STOP PAYING FOR COFFEE, TEA, AND SHAKES – SERIOUSLY.

Make your own coffee, tea, and shakes! There's absolutely no excuse not to make a budget-friendly homemade alternative for your favorite morning beverage ritual. At first, I invested in a Nespresso coffee machine. I did the math and found that it would take me less than five months for the machine to pay for itself in savings. But eventually, I realized that I could make three days worth of cold brew overnight, and the beans are incredibly cheap. Plus, making your own coffee is fresher, has a more robust taste, and saves you from being tempted to add on that sausage breakfast sandwich or cake pop at the cafe. As I laid out earlier, by skipping that daily $4 latte (plus $1 tip!), you're giving yourself the gift of *$1,300 in savings* each year.

> **Frankie's Finer Points**: Try roasting your own beans. With a little investment up front towards a roaster, you can order green beans online for around $2 or less per pound. Home-roasted beans make an excellent gift (think housewarming, Christmas for coworkers) and you might find yourself a fun new hobby that's dark on beans and light on the wallet!

31 COMMIT TO ENTERTAINMENT ON THE CHEAP – OR FREE!

Let's talk entertainment. Did you know there's an iTunes section for 99 cent movie rentals? Sometimes you'll even find your favorite videos to own for just $5.99 (great if it's something you know you'll want to watch over and over again). Just like you can share Netflix subscriptions, if you have a friend with an HBO or Hulu account, ask if they're willing to share their login.

Even better, try the app Reelgood: it lets you enter the streaming services you have access to, and then you can search for entertainment all in one place. You can look for popular shows on your platforms, or search for a specific title and it'll help you find it for free!

Another way to watch movies on the cheap? Some local theaters (at least in Seattle) have weekly specials. Check out their websites and you might find deals on Monday shows before 6 pm for example, or other ways to see a $5 new release. Perk: you're might even have a little extra elbow room around you!

Another way to save on entertainment? Join your local library! It's an amazing FREE resource. Use it. You'll never be tempted to splurge on another book again. Even if the book you want is in use, you can request it at your local library and get notified by email when it arrives. Depending on where you live, it usually only takes 7-10 days even for the most popular books. Just be wary of late fees; those can add up if you have a lot checked out, so don't overdo it. Oh, and did I mention you can also rent TV shows and movies from the library? You can also download Kindle ebooks straight to your device! Not only are you saving money, but you're supporting a local resource that helps your community thrive! *Pat on the back*

32 CLOTHES: THRIFTING, TAILORING, & REPAIRING.

There are some pretty trendy thrift shops these days (thanks, Macklemore!). Do a quick web search in your neighborhood and check some out! Locally, I frequent Buffalo Exchange and Plato's Closet. Don't overlook Goodwill too for some one-of-a-kind finds from a place that also does great things for your community.

Are you and a friend both tired of your own closets? Try a clothes swap! For special occasions, pay a little to get that old suit or dress fixed, trimmed, or slimmed. New suits cost $400, $500 minimum – have it tailored for $50 instead. Repair those old heels instead of buying new. Just don't break them again the next time you do the Electric Slide! Savings – *"it's electric!"*

33 TRY THESE TIPS FOR SHOPPING.

Shopping online? Never ever pay for shipping. Don't have Amazon Prime? Find a friend that does! Find shipping loopholes for your favorite stores. Here's an example: Macy's gives you free shipping if you add a "beauty item" to your order. I found a $2 avocado face mask stocking stuffer for my girlfriend that saved me $8 on shipping. Also, give yourself 24 hours between putting items in your cart and purchasing – this exercise will help you curb retail therapy.

Going out? Are you shopping somewhere where you know you're likely to make some impulse buys? Try this trick: pass up putting that tempting item in your cart. Continue your shopping. If you're *still* thinking about that item when you get to check out, go back and get it. But chances are you will have totally forgotten... at least until you get home when it's too late. This works especially well at Target (*Oh, that knock-off coat!*), Costco (*Set of new cutting boards for $20?!*), and grocery stores (*giant squash, just 5 for $10!*).

> **Frankie's Finer Points**: Don't grab a shopping cart at all. Do an entire lap around the store taking photos (including price) of everything you're thinking of buying. When you're done, swipe through them and make your decisions. Yes, it takes more time, but time is money when you're making or saving it! I found this tip is especially useful at warehouse stores when looking for a gift.

34 BE SUSTAINABLE AND FRUGAL.

As a classic example of a Seattle citizen, my resolution this year (along with continuing my financial independence journey of course) is to try to make environmentally sustainable choices whenever possible. Wouldn't you know, this goal works hand-in-hand with building financial wealth! Here are some quick hits:

- Try commuting via bike instead of driving yourself. Not only does this produce zero emissions, but it's *completely free*! If that sounds like too big of a change, challenge yourself to find an alternative commute method just once a week and add in more days throughout the year.
- I researched and found out, Seattle charges $74.30/mo for a 64-gallon garbage can collection, and $23.30/mo for a 12-gallon can. Not only can you save *$612 a year* on TRASH, but that's over 600 gallons of garbage that you can choose to not put in a landfill. If you don't have jurisdiction over your trash collection (especially fellow apartment dwellers), try reducing other utilities: using less water, electricity, and gas all have huge impacts on your monthly bills.
- Give Meatless Mondays a try! Did you know that if everyone on earth ate vegetarian for just one day every week (which, by the way, is incredibly easy), we could reduce greenhouse gas emissions by an amount *equivalent to taking 273 million cars off the road*[10]? Not only would you make an environmental impact, but just think about that $3/lb of ground beef versus the $1.50/lb of dried beans (which, by the way, will make you *12 servings*) – those are some huge savings!

Extra Credit: Forgo alcohol.

I'm adding this tip in as a bonus because it may not pertain to everyone, just those of us that like to have a drink after a hard day's work. And sometimes while cooking... and sometimes with dinner... and one to wind down after dinner. Alcohol is a great treat, but it's definitely a drain on the bank account. Try forgoing drinking alcohol for most days every week, and instead, treat yourself to some serious savings. A tip from my newlywed friends: they make simple mocktails almost every night as a way to feel fancy and not miss the booze.

6

INVESTING

"If you're still doing what mommy and daddy said for you to do (go to school, get a job, and save money), you're losing." - *Robert Kiyosaki*

While saving is good, investing is better. You can't frugal your way to riches in retirement. In fact, it's nearly impossible to save your way to retirement alone. For example, if you set aside $1,000 a month in cash and stashed it away in a zero interest account (aka the safe in your basement), it would take you more than 82 years to save one million dollars – which is the minimum recommended nest egg for most people to retire. Instead, investing the same amount of money into an investment account would net you over one million dollars in about 28 years.

Compound interest (when your interest makes interest) makes all the difference. Not to mention, the sooner you start investing, the more your return will be. There are tons of anecdotes and scenarios that outline the benefit of investing early in your life: basically, the longer you wait, the harder it will be to reach your financial goals.

You might look at all your debt and think you don't have any money left to invest. All I can say is #PayYourselfFirst. That means you need to allocate a percentage of your pay to an emergency fund, longer-term investments, your retirement account, and even a travel fund before you throw it all at your bills and debts. If you pay yourself last, you'll never get ahead. Trust me. It's recommended that you set aside at least 20% of your take-home pay for savings. That's only about an hour and a half of your 8-hour work day going towards yourself and your future. Future you will thank you.

35 UNDERSTAND THE (POWERFUL) CONCEPT OF COMPOUND INTEREST AND THE RULE OF 72.

Compound interest can be an extremely powerful factor for building wealth and an essential concept to understand – especially for those a bit apprehensive about dipping their toes into the stock market. Simply put, according to Investopedia compound interest is the interest an investor earns on their original investment plus all the interest earned on the interest that has accumulated over time. That's a mouthful. Essentially, it's earning interest ON your interest year after year. The longer you allow your money to grow, the more compounded, or exponential, your returns will be.

With that said, let's figure out how I came up with that comparison math between saving and investing in the intro: how long would it take you to become a millionaire using the power of compound interest if you were to invest $1,000 a month at a rate of 7% interest (a conservative estimate of the rate of return that the S&P 500 earns historically)? Let's dissect a complicated, fancy algorithm that I'll breakdown into 137 simple steps... Kidding. Use NerdWallet's Compound Interest Calculator instead. The answer: in this scenario, you would earn one million dollars in less than 28 years.

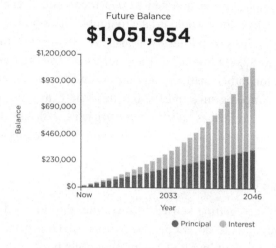

Future Balance
$1,051,954

Source: Compound Interest Calculator[11], NerdWallet

How about two million? Just over 36 years. Three million? 42 years. For comparison, if you saved $1,000 a month at zero interest for 42 years? Just $505,000 George Washingtons. Yes, that 7% return compounded over time would have earned you about 6x more over 42 years. #MindBlown.

Okay, so investing $1,000 a month might not sound realistic for everyone. But even $250 invested monthly over 28 years with the same annual return of 7% would net you more than $260,000 (compared to just $84,000 if you didn't invest at all). Play around with the Compound Interest Calculator to see how different scenarios stack up – it just might be the push you need to start investing.

This brings us to another important concept in investing: The Rule of 72. This is a simple formula that helps you estimate how long it would take you to double an investment. To use the rule, you take 72 and divide it by your rate of growth (interest).

For example, if you invested $1,000 today and it earned 7% annually, how long would it take to double? It's simple. Take 72 and divide it by 7: it'll take you just over 10 years to turn this $1,000 to $2,000 if you set it and forget it. This isn't an exact science (or rather math) by any means and it doesn't take into account ongoing investments, but this rule helps you identify investment timelines quickly and efficiently. Alright, enough math, theory, and brain-busters. Let's get back to taking action!

36 CREATE AN ACORNS ACCOUNT.

If you're just getting started in investing, the first and easiest thing you should do is open an Acorns account. After a little setup, this way of investing is almost entirely hands-off. Acorns is an online service that (for just $1 a month) will round up all your purchases via a linked debit or credit card to the nearest dollar and invest that change for you. You can also change the settings to round up by 2x, 3x, or even 10x. Once it's up and running, don't peek and instead just go about making purchases like you normally would. After a few months, take a look and you'll be surprised at how your pennies, nickels, and dimes have grown! Using Acorns is a great way to save effortlessly for something specific, like a trip, since you really don't notice the change leaving your wallet. But I personally recommend you set it and forget it – forever! (Because compounding interest, of course). Of all the "FinTech" (financial technology) I spent time with in 2018, Acorns stood above the rest for its ease of use and simplicity. Looking back, I accumulated *exactly* $969.46 on 1,122 round-ups in my first year using Acorns.

37 OPEN A ROTH IRA.

A Roth IRA (Individual Retirement Account, and today I

learned named after Senator William Roth of Delaware) is a personal retirement account that you fund with your post-tax income. What this means is that you've already paid the taxes upfront so when you withdraw your earnings at age 59 ½ you will not have to pay any taxes on the principal money invested – it's a gift to future you!

Almost all brokerage firms offer IRAs, and you can invest your contributions in many ways (stocks, mutual funds, bonds, and even CDs). An important note is that while you will be fined for taking out your investment earnings before that 59 ½ retirement benchmark, you can withdraw the *contributions* that you made at any time, penalty free. This actually makes a Roth IRA an excellent vehicle if you're planning to buy a home, fund higher education, or even just as an emergency fund.

I opened my Roth IRA through the online broker TD Ameritrade in a matter of minutes. In 2018, the annual limit for an IRA was $5,500 and in 2019 it will be $6,000. Try to hit this max!

38 START YOUR OWN TRADITIONAL IRA.

A traditional IRA is essentially the same as a Roth IRA except for one key difference: unlike a Roth IRA, with a traditional IRA, you'll pay taxes when you withdraw the funds in retirement. The benefit of contributing to a traditional IRA is that your contributions are tax-deductible for your current tax year (meaning you are eligible to save on your tax return), but you will owe taxes anytime you take any of this money out.

Yes, you can open your own traditional IRA even if you participate in a work 401(k) plan and the contribution limits for the two are separate. You can also have both a traditional IRA and a Roth IRA, but $6,000 is the annual limit to how much you can contribute to both of these IRAs *combined* in 2019. I recommend you do a little research yourself to understand the key differences between a traditional and Roth if you're considering your own IRA, and to see what best fits your tax situation.

Keep in mind that you cannot withdraw from a traditional IRA before 59 ½ without (in most cases) facing a 10% penalty, in addition to being taxed on this income. Personally, I opened my traditional IRA through Betterment and set up auto payments on the 1st and 15th of each month to coincide with my pay schedule. For 2019, I decided to put $5,000 in my Roth and $1,000 in my traditional IRA because right now I prefer to have my funds available with no withdrawal fee. I may reconsider my IRA allocations in future years as life circumstances change.

39 DABBLE (AND ONLY DABBLE) IN INDIVIDUAL STOCKS.

Buying individual stocks is a dangerous game and typically not a smart way to count on growing your wealth. So, it may seem counterintuitive that I'm going to tell you to play a game you'll probably lose, but hear me out. A super easy and relatively low-risk way to try out the stock market for your first time is with an app like Stockpile or Robinhood. Both have super low fees and you can buy partial amounts of stock for a few bucks, which is great when desirable stocks like Tesla and Alphabet will currently set you back $300-$1,000 for each share. Don't want to use real money? Set up an account with TD Ameritrade and use their "paperMoney" feature to invest fake dollars in your favorite companies and see what happens historically over time without consequence.

Best of luck, but you'll likely lose (and if you don't, let's chat...). You'll almost never beat the market if you buy individual stocks but it might take going through the exercise to convince yourself to never pick individual stocks again. To be clear, here is my real advice regarding the stock market: never invest in individual stocks. Even experts rarely best the market. If you do dabble with real money, use a very small amount and I highly suggest you pull out at +/- 5% either way.

Here's what happened when I experimented (with real dollars):

Using Stockpile, I purchased $50 worth of stock each in 3 companies I liked: Apple, Amazon, and Nintendo. After some small initial returns, I was feeling ambitious and so I bought $50 of Netflix. This one took off in mid-2018. Suddenly, my $200 investment had grown about $50 in two months. Color me happy! *This is how I'll get rich! I'm totally good at this*! No. No, I'm not. Over the next several months I bought stocks with $50 here and there when I could. Eventually, I ended up with fractions of shares in a dozen companies. Flash forward to late December 2018. My $500 I invested was down 6.64%, and that's *excluding* purchase fees and transfer fees for moving money into the app. It would have been so much wiser to just put that $500 into an IRA or invest in ETFs (see next step!) and sit back while it gained an average 7% rate of return. Chalk this one up as a lesson learned.

40 INVEST IN ETFS AND MUTUAL FUNDS.

ETFs (exchange-traded funds) and mutual funds are both professionally managed groupings of stocks and/or bonds. They are less risky than investing in individual stocks as they are professionally developed and overseen to make sure they stay on target. There are some key differences between the two, so research and see what makes the most sense for your goals.

Eventually, aim to put the majority of your investments in

ETFs and/or mutual funds. Companies I've mentioned before (e.g. Betterment, Wealthfront, your IRA provider) can invest your money via a diversified portfolio of ETFs and mutual funds. You can bet on the entire stock market with safe and inexpensive (fee-wise) Vanguard ETFs like VOO or VTI.

Personally, I used TD Ameritrade to invest in ETFs and mutual funds. I also balance these with bonds and other less volatile investments. With mutual funds, you can automate your investments so you're not waiting for a downturn in the market to jump in – this is referred to as "dollar cost averaging." You can also invest in target-date retirement funds which automatically lessened your investment risk over time as you move closer to the date (usually anticipated retirement) that you want to access the money.

Set up an investment plan that works for you. Peek at your returns if you must, but do not react either way (i.e. panic and sell everything when they're low). I can't stress this point enough. The best way to let your money grow with compound interest is to set it and forget it.

Note: Please do your own research when picking ETFs and mutual funds or making any investment decisions.

41 GET OUT OF (OR TOTALLY AVOID) CRYPTOCURRENCY AND BITCOIN.

Delete the app. Remove the saved blog site. Pull the movies out of your Netflix queue. Just run. This was where I started my financial journey: I invested $150 over 3 coins via the app Coinbase at the "peak" of the cryptocurrency craze in January 2018. When their value dropped below $100 I told myself I'd pull out when it hit $100 again. It didn't. I lost big time. I came away with only \$38 of my initial investment, and that's not including any transaction fees. Why did I try Bitcoin? It was all the rage, of course. Started with Mashable articles, developed into Netflix documentaries. Plus, that story about 50 Cent... Avoid the noise and just *stay away*.

7

WORK & MAKING WORK WORK
FOR YOU

There are two types of people in the world: those who like their job, and those who do not. (Oh, and those who make huge generalizations about types of people.) Whichever category you fall into, there are still smart and easy ways to make your work work for you.

42 UPDATE YOUR LINKEDIN.

No, your boss won't notice and assume you're looking for a new job. If you're unhappy at work but not ready to throw in the towel without a solid backup plan – get on LinkedIn. Even if you are happy at work, create a network on LinkedIn that will support and endorse you when you're ready for your next promotion. Make connections. Find people with a similar career history and see what kind of jobs they've had and explored. Look up companies that you admire and "follow" them. Make nice with all the many recruiters and let them help you find your next job. You'll never know what's out there unless you look – and there's a *lot* out there. If you do land a job offer but are on the fence, take the offer back to your boss and use it as leverage to negotiate a new title or more pay. Either way, up your LinkedIn game. It's worth the effort and it's the only networking site I use.

43 ASK FOR A RAISE.

Seriously. This is the easiest and fastest way to build your wealth and all it takes is a conversation. Don't simply recite your current tasks to demonstrate your value. Highlight your accomplishments, reiterate your dedication to the company, and call out any upcoming initiatives and new projects that you will positively contribute to. Contribute to company culture in a concrete way? Sneak in a subtle reminder. Don't sound ungrateful. Don't make threats. Have an open and honest conversation about the value you bring to your company, and state your worth. It's important to stay calm and even practice if you have to – so emotions don't take over.

> **Frankie's Finer Points**: Don't love your current job? Shop around for an upgrade! Research shows that people who stay with their employer longer than two years get paid on average 50% less in their lifetime[12]. Think about it. The *best* employees can hope for annual raises of 3-5%. When you switch to a new employer, you have the opportunity to increase your salary by 10-20% right off the top, not to mention the potential for signing bonuses and stock options if you play your cards right.

44 USE ALL OF YOUR BONUSES TO PAY OFF DEBT OR BILLS.

Get a bonus from work? Put *all* of it towards your credit card or another outstanding bill. It's tempting to see this windfall as "free money" and blow it all on a vacation or new car.

Here's where it's important to remember your goals – once you have a handle on your expenses, sure, put a portion of your bonus towards something fun! But for now, focus on your why.

> **Frankie's Finer Points**: Do you get paid every other week? Here's some fun advice: divide your annual pay into 24 pay cycles (instead of 26) when you're budgeting. Most months, you'll have one payday early in the month and another towards the end. But, twice a year, you'll have *three* paydays that month. That extra payday will feel like a hefty bonus! You'll have a full, unbudgeted paycheck to put towards one of your goals, without disrupting your monthly routine.

45 UP YOUR 401(K) CONTRIBUTION.

If your company offers an employer match to your 401(k), start there. That's simply free money you're leaving on the table, otherwise. Up your contribution by 1% every month, aiming for the annual max of $19,000 (as of 2019). Upping your contribution can be relatively straightforward. It might require a simple form or could be as easy as a few clicks in your retirement portal online. If maxing out sounds impossible in the first year, make a goal to get to a 12% contribution (or double your current strategy, or anything similar that makes sense for you) and make hitting the annual max a 2-year goal instead. Don't forget, your retirement savings have to account for inflation so you absolutely must set your personal goal aggressively. Note: employer contributions are *not* included in the $19,000 annual limit.

What if your company doesn't provide a match? I would actually recommend you skip the 401(k) and first max out a Roth IRA instead. Once you do that, now go back and contribute as much as possible to your 401(k). Read step #37 for more information about the benefits of a Roth IRA.

> **Frankie's Finer Points**: A new company Blooom (three o's, not a typo) will automatically help you optimize your retirement portfolio for $10 a month. Even without a paid subscription, they also offer a free analysis of your current employer-sponsored retirement plan to help you discover hidden fees.

46 SPEND TIME TO FULLY UNDERSTAND YOUR HEALTH BENEFITS.

There's really a lot to unpack here but, the reality is, this one is going to be up to you to tackle on your own because benefits are uniquely different at every company. The best advice I can give is to ask questions. Like, a lot of them. Often times, companies keep a 1 to 2-sheet summary quickly highlighting the key benefits available to their employees. That's a great starting point. If that's not available, ask your Human Resources department where all the benefits paperwork lives (generally on an intranet or internal work site). Spend a weekend really digging through it all and, again, ask questions! Shoot some emails back and forth or, if you want, set up a meeting with HR to get some 1:1 attention. I'm always surprised how quickly I hear back from HR and how eager they are to help!

So what should you be looking for when sorting through your benefit options and opportunities? For starters, if you have health benefits, be sure you're on a plan that makes the most sense for you. Don't just choose the plan with the lowest premium or the cheapest copay: make sure you're taking into account if you have any existing health concerns that require a specific provider, or if you're someone who visits the doctor frequently or hardly ever.

Some plans with a high-deductible offer benefits like a

health savings account (HSA) which can actually have huge savings and even investing benefits (more on HSAs in a moment) – so don't necessarily ignore those plans because they seem expensive. Really dig in and try to understand the pros and cons of your different options. Even if you find you're happy with your plans and don't need to make any changes now, it's always great to know what your options are for when open enrollment comes around or life situations inevitably change.

Here are some other quick tips for understanding your work benefits:

- If you're starting a new job, ask for the PowerPoint that was presented to you on Day 1 regarding employee benefit plans.
- Create accounts (if you haven't) with all your benefit providers and poke around their sites.
- If you're able to find all the HR benefit paperwork, print it all and organize the documents into a handy folder that you can open up and dig through on a rainy weekend (aka every weekend here in Seattle!).
- If you're married and both employed, be sure to compare plans. I have a friend who is offered fine health insurance through work, but if she opts out she gets a massive stipend (aka pay increase) instead. So, she declines her work's insurance policy and instead is covered by her spouse for cheap. Also be sure to coordinate with your spouse on life and AD&D (accidental death and dismemberment) insurance if your work provides it – you'll want to make sure you're both looking out for each other if worst comes to worst.

- Beyond the typical benefits like health insurance and retirement account options, be sure to see if your work provides other perks or discounts on common expenses like transportation, fitness, cell phone providers, or childcare.

47 TAKE ADVANTAGE OF YOUR HSA AND FSA.

Do not gloss over this step if your company provides this opportunity. Understanding the differences between an HSA (Health Savings Account) and FSA (Flexible Spending Account) and learning how to use an HSA to invest was one of the biggest ah-ha moments of the year for me.

Let's start simple. First, here's how they are similar. Both HSAs and FSAs are tax-advantaged accounts that allow people to save untaxed money towards medical expenses. To be eligible for an HSA, you must be on a high-deductible health plan (HDHP). That is, you'll have to cover $1,350 or more annually of out-of-pocket health-related expenses before your benefits kick in. An FSA, on the other hand, does not have any eligibility qualifications other than being available through your employer. Both have limits regarding how much pretax money you can set aside for each annually (in short: HSA option allows you to set aside more).

Both of these options usually come with a debit card linked to your HSA or FSA that you can use towards eligible medical expenses (even at Rite Aid when buying band-aids, glasses, and aspirin for example). Be sure you always have this card on you, and activated! Log in to the website and track your account balance much like you would your own checking account.

One key difference between the two is that any unused HSA funds rollover each year. With an FSA, it's use it or lose it. Same goes with getting a new job: your HSA remains yours while your FSA would typically be lost. Another difference: in an

HSA, funds become available as you add money to the account while in an FSA, the money you elect to contribute each year is available immediately in full.

So which to choose? As with all things finance, you should do your own research to make an educated decision that works best for your situation. Personally, I went with the HSA which means I have an HDHP and have to cover up to $2,500 of medical expenses out-of-pocket annually – which I can just pay with the HSA! I decided to max out my pre-tax savings ($3,450 in 2018) AND invest funds in the account over $1,000. Yes, you can do that! For me, this was the ah-ha moment. This functions much like a 401(k) but towards your health. The money grows tax-free with compounding interest potentially for decades, until you really, really need it in old age. Did you know the number one expense in retirement is health care? Sure, it's a little money now, but with the power of compound interest, this invested money can grow exponentially for years. With your health care benefits and this money socked away, you might not even have to pay an out-of-pocket dime the day your first child is born!

If you go with an FSA, here are a couple quick tips:

- Make sure to sign up each year for a realistic amount that you think you'll actually need for healthcare expenses. Track last year's spending as a starting point or amp up the contribution if you know you'll need a major surgery this year, for example.
- If the end of the year is coming and you still have funds left, stock up your first aid kit or other common household medical supplies at your local pharmacy. Not sure what qualifies? FSA Store's website has a handy list tells you everything you can and can not

cover with your FSA. Or, plan an extra dental
cleaning or check-up before year end!

There are plenty more things you should know about HSAs
and FSAs including why you should keep receipts and how you
can pay yourself back at any time, sending money straight to
your personal bank accounts. NBS benefits has an article[13] that
covers the basics well!

8

MAKING EXTRA MONEY

"Money is not everything. Make sure you earn a lot before speaking such nonsense." - Warren Buffett

The best way to reach your financial goals? Duh, make more money faster! In all seriousness though, there are so many ways to make money beyond your regular paycheck. If you can add one or two of these cash makers to your repertoire, you could bring in a couple extra hundred dollars each month or more!

48 START A SIDE HUSTLE.

There are countless ways to make some extra cash outside your 9 to 5. Some call it their "5 to 9". Even if you work different hours, you can use your spare time on a side hustle. Here are some ideas to jump-start your brainstorm:

- Join Instacart and become a personal grocery shopper
- Drive for Uber or Lyft

- Start a YouTube channel or a blog and learn to monetize
- Write an eBook on a subject you're passionate about (I know someone who did this!)
- Offer a skill on sites like Fiverr or Upwork
- Walk dogs via Rover or Wag! or post an advertisement with permission at nearby apartments
- Get paid to do chores with TaskRabbit
- Look on Craigslist for temporary gigs in your area (e.g. babysitting, special event staff)
- Love taking great photos? Sell stock photography

You might be surprised how easy it is to make active and passive income on the side. If you have skills and some free time, make some extra paper!

49 SELL THINGS YOU HAVE AROUND THE HOUSE.

There are lots of ways to sell your gently used items. Personally, I prefer Craigslist – it's free and you don't have to bother with shipping. I've also sold my records and physical video games (don't buy digital copies! You can't resell those!) to friends at work. If I know of a friend who is moving, I might offer a fair price on some of my extra furniture or household items I have tucked away. There are tons of methods to try out, and you'd be surprised what people will buy – one man's trash is another man's treasure! Bonus: It opens up space in your closet or storage unit, and when it comes to stuff (aka clutter), less is always more.

Be sure to be safe when using Craigslist. I use an alternate email address when posting ads to not only stay organized but also to keep my real information private. Meet in public well-lit places, and never give out your address or phone number. Bring a friend too if that helps you feel comfortable. Also, agree on a price ahead of time or you might waste your time with someone trying to lowball you – don't allow any haggling on the spot unless they have a valid point (like a missing or broken component).

50 SELL CLOTHES.

Here's something most of you can try this weekend for some quick cash:

- **Friday night:** start organizing your unwanted clothes into two piles: donate and sell. Make sure everything is clean and semi-unwrinkled.
- **Saturday:** take the sell pile to a thrift store, like Buffalo Exchange, that buys used clothing. Don't be tempted by the store credit offer (unless you are already intending to shop for clothes) and opt for cash. Then, take the items that they didn't buy and repeat at another thrift store.
- **Sunday:** take your donate pile and leftovers from the sell pile to Goodwill. At the end of the weekend, you'll have made a nice bit of cash and you can feel good about donating your leftover duds and cleaning up your closet!

If you enjoy selling clothes, reach out to friends or family and do it with their clothes! Most won't want money in exchange – you're doing them a favor by saving them time and space. Plus, they'll feel all the charitable feels when what you can't sell reaches a Goodwill in the end.

P.S. I know what you're thinking: "This guy knows how

to have a wild weekend!" You're right. You should see me now editing this book on a Saturday night!

51 FLIP ITEMS FOR EXTRA CASH.

Flipping is simple: you sell something for more money than you paid for it. Visit your local flea market or thrift store. In the summer, hit up garage sales (why isn't there a better app for finding these?!). Look around for hidden treasures that are underpriced and sell them yourself at a profit. If you wait until the last day of a yard sale, it's especially easy to haggle as the owner just wants to clear everything out! When you find a potential item, don't be scared to pull out your phone on the spot to research if you think you found something valuable! When it comes time to sell, post your item on Craigslist, OfferUp, eBay, or a local swap shop if you have that resource.

You can hunt Craigslist or OfferUp for your flip finds, but it can be a bit more work. Make sure you know the product well. Here's a recent personal flip story: after setting up an alert in Craigslist, I received a notification about a Wii U plus five games listed for $120. I offered $100, and we settled on $105 – I knew this was a total steal and this college student seller seemed eager to part with it. Two days later, I sold three of the games in a bundle for $15 each. Two weeks later, I sold the rest of the bundle for...drum roll please... $120. That's $60 of pure and easy profit, but it did require some time. You better believe I splurged on fancy sourdough bread that week for my lunch sandwiches!

52 JOIN A PAID ONLINE SURVEY COMMUNITY.

This one is super simple although it's certainly not a "get rich quick" scheme. There are tons of sites (I like Survey Junkie) that will pay you for your opinions. This is great if you're just watching TV or winding down before bed. A survey generally only takes a few minutes to complete and you can expect anywhere from 25 cents to $2.50 each. Don't expect to make more than $10 every couple of weeks, but the surveys can be fun and a little extra cash is never a bad thing. I've been a Survey Junkie member for a few months and have made a total of $41.50. Memorable surveys thus far have been about Dominoes, car commercials, and my political beliefs – pretty fun stuff!

Frankie's Finer Points: If they're available in your area, join survey communities User Research International and Fieldwork. These are market research companies that will send you emails about paid research studies in your area. Just a few weeks ago, I signed up for a video game study that was scheduled for a full Saturday at Microsoft headquarters and would pay $300 cash – sounded like a good time! I made my way over to Microsoft, helped myself to their stocked fridge and a free coffee, waited about an hour, and then was told that they had overbooked the study and I could leave... *while still being paid the full $300.* Best day ever.

9

INSURANCE

This chapter could be entitled, "helping you sleep at night." In my financial clean-up journey of 2018, I learned there are some insurance must-haves that I didn't have and I also learned there are some policies that I could've lived without. Plus, sorting out my insurance was honestly super easy: I tackled all of the steps below in a week during my lunch breaks. The reality is, accidents are a part of life. I've been through several myself – like the time someone, likely inspired by Beyoncé's Lemonade, vandalized the sh** out of my car just to steal a bag of clothes ready for Goodwill from the backseat... But, that doesn't mean disasters and accidents have to set us back financially. The right insurance can turn a mountain into a molehill. Plus, did I mention I *love* sleep?

53 LOWER YOUR CAR INSURANCE BILL.

I have a confession. I was paying too much for car insurance and didn't even realize it. Luckily, I got this notification from Mint telling me the bad news:

Even if you think your policy is a steal, shop around for multiple car insurance quotes. Call your current provider and ask them to match the lowest rate you find or you'll switch companies. If they won't match that quote... switch!

Pay the largest installment (fancy word for *bill payment*) you can. Companies usually incentivize paying more upfront with lower rates and/or fewer fees. For example, if you can afford to pay an entire year of your policy up front, do it! You can save up to 10% by doing so. Even paying 6 months up front can save you up to 5%. Plus, then you can strike that monthly expense from your budget which will free up your pay. Geico even spells it out clearly on their website: *If you elect to pay your premium in installments, each installment may be subject to an additional charge.*

Digging deeper in my Geico portal, I found that the best way to save was to enroll in Electronic Funds Transfer (EFT), aka linking my bank account for autopay. By paying off my bill each month by entering card information, I would be billed an installment charge of $5 for each payment. However, by electing to pay using EFT, the fee is reduced to $1. While fees are never fun and ideally should always be avoided, this one is a no-brainer. If I opt to pay each month with a card, rather than autopay I would be charged $60 a year on the monthly payment plan (12 months x $5 = $60) rather than $12 a year using EFT (12 months x $1 = $12). Ultimately, the best way for me to save is to pay at least 6 months at a time via EFT. This example is specific to Geico so be sure to fully understand your payment and plan options if you're with a different provider.

Frankie's Finer Points: If you're able to bundle several insurance policies (see my other recommended insurances below) with one company, you'll save.

54 SPRING FOR RENTERS INSURANCE.

Yes, this costs money... but renters insurance can be as cheap as $8-10 a month for total peace of mind. Some landlords even require it. Once you sign up, be sure to take photos and even videos of all your possessions in the event that a disaster does happen. Personally, my policy is through State Farm and I pay my bill 6-months at a time for extra savings. Ask around for quotes and again, be sure to compare your options.

Note: I'm assuming you don't own your home and if you do, you have home insurance as a given. My only advice then would be to shop for the best rates.

55 GET LIFE INSURANCE.

No, life insurance isn't a scam, and again, it'll give you peace of mind. There are two basic types: term and whole life insurance[14]. In short, term life insurance is cheaper each month but has an "expiration date" in that the payout benefit is only valid for a predetermined length of time (usually 10, 20, or 30 years). Whole life insurance tends to be more expensive monthly, but the policy is good for as long as you're alive. With both types, you name a beneficiary or beneficiaries who you want to receive a sum of money in the event that the worst happens...

Some employers offer free life insurance but the beneficiary payout for those policies are usually in the range of $50K. Sadly, that's hardly enough to help your loved ones cover loss-of-life expenses, which I won't dig into because that's depressing... NerdWallet has an excellent article on The Differences Between Term and Whole Life Insurance – read through and see what will work best for you.

I enrolled in a $250K 30-year term life insurance policy through Haven Life for roughly $20 a month. They claim it takes minutes to enroll, and that's no lie: it took about 10 minutes from start to finish.

56 QUALIFY FOR INSURANCE DISCOUNTS.

Tell your insurance company about any steps you've taken to improve your insurability. What does this even mean? With some insurers, you can get discounts for all kinds of things like pursuing higher education, installing home security cameras (yes, even inexpensive indoor ones), and even driving less. Start the conversation and see what discount opportunities your provider offers.

Frankie's Finer Points: If you are successful at lowering your car insurance (I slashed mine by almost 30%, for example) and getting discounts, the savings from those activities alone could easily cover the cost of adding renters and life insurance.

57 AVOID CERTAIN INSURANCE OPTIONS.

There are some insurance policies out there that are an absolute waste of your money. Don't pay for rental car insurance, U-Haul accident/damage insurance, phone insurance, Best Buy Geek Squad fancy-pancy 2-year support insurance, or things similar. All you need is auto, home/renters, and life. Did you know, certain credit cards will automatically cover your car rental and U-Haul coverage for you? Some even offer purchase protection on big-ticket items like electronics. Read the fine print or give your credit card company a call and ask. Or, consider shopping around for a new credit card that provides the types of coverage that are important to you. First, see Chapter 4 on Credit Cards for more information.

10

INVEST IN YOURSELF

"Whether you think you can or think you can't, you're right."
Henry Ford

Often, people are looking for that quick win that'll bring them big, guaranteed returns (hello, Powerball) but the reality is, no investment is ever a guarantee. However, investing in yourself is one purchase that won't give you buyer's remorse if you do it the right way. I've watched countless YouTube videos about ~the best ways to invest X amount of money~ and nearly all of them suggest investing in yourself – it's an important concept! Some of the to-dos in this section are intentionally left a little vague because it's ultimately up to you to decide what investing in yourself will look like.

58 INVEST IN HOME COMPUTING – ON THE CHEAP!

After selling my 5-year old MacBook Pro a couple years ago, I went years relying solely on an original iPad Mini. The reality is, an iPad Mini was not helping me achieve productivity and even the top model iPad Pro probably wouldn't. For many years, I assumed the only alternative was buying a brand new, soon-to-be-outdated $2,000 laptop but I just couldn't justify the cost.

Enter: Chromebook. I decided to buy this as my first new "laptop" in 10 years after reading many positive reviews and finding a great deal at Costco which included a mouse, all on sale for around $225! A year later, it has more than paid for itself in helping me budget, research credit cards, find the best travel deals, track my goals, work from home, and more. While I can wholeheartedly recommend the Acer 14" Chromebook, you should spend time assessing what technology will help you be successful in your financial goals.

59 UPGRADE YOUR KITCHEN.

In the past, my mindset about food was that since eating was essential, it must be essential to always eat great food – which often meant delivery or dining out on the regular. The reality is, nothing beats a good home-cooked meal. From price to taste to the social aspects of cooking with friends: a homemade meal checks all the boxes!

But, if you're like me, starting a daily cooking ritual can be a daunting challenge. I quickly learned that all it takes is the right tools to not only get inspired but to successfully execute good dishes. If home is where the heart is, and the kitchen is the heart of the home, then… well I don't know but dammit get in there and cook and you'll find out. Here's my list of no-regrets kitchen items I invested in that will last many a meal:

- Quality knife block set & chopping knives
- Quality pots & pans set
- Measuring cups & mixing bowls
- Blender & immersion blender

- Plates & bowls
- Good olive oil & spices in bulk
- Ample storage options for leftovers

Frankie's Finer Points: Cook more than you need and don't waste a scrap. Pack leftovers for lunch the next day (and maybe even the next!) because it'll save you money AND your awesome sauce still tastes awesome the next day. Jimmy John's is fast and cheap; leftovers are faster and free! Hey, I should put that on a shirt!

60 LOVE YOUR HOME.

Surround yourself with what sparks joy (#MarieKondo, amirite?). Even if you might not think you're creative, here are some simple tips to make any home your personal oasis:

- Paint an accent wall in the living room or bedroom
- Organize your books or records by color
- Hang or display pictures and art
- Create a space for YOU: an office, a nook, or a ~~man cave~~ den
- Hang fun lights inside and out – lights can do wonders for mood
- Remove the clutter in your closet, in your kitchen, and in your entryway

Having a welcoming home positively impacts your mood and productivity – especially if you work from home or will be spending more time at home "getting it together" financially (e.g. hosting friends and eating in). Create and develop an environment that inspires and stimulates you. I've found less is generally more and small, inexpensive projects can really go a long way for a great mood.

61 CONTINUE LEARNING ONLINE AND IN YOUR COMMUNITY.

There are lots of great places on the web to help you gain new knowledge or expand an existing skill set. Sites like Udemy, Coursera, and Lynda have courses on just about any topic that you can think of for cheap (and in some cases free). I've taken courses to brush up on Excel, marketing, and Photoshop.

There are also inexpensive ways to learn in your community. Attend a local lecture on a college campus for free. Go to a City Hall event (I pick up the quarterly calendar at my local library). Go to a book reading at your local bookstore. Try out a cooking class at your local market. Get your intro level sommelier certificate. Join a Toastmasters club and practice public speaking. Spend time and a little money on making you a happier, smarter, more powerful you. Skills and certificates make YOU more valuable.

62 START A RAINY DAY FUND (AND USE IT ON A NEW HOBBY).

Many of us want to try a new hobby. Some of us probably even set a resolution to start one up in this new year. However, it's easy to give up when you can't come up with the startup funds required to dive in. Painting requires paint brushes and paint. Rock climbers need shoes and gear. Knitting requires needles and yarns. If you want to learn to ski, gear, lift tickets, and lessons are downright expensive.

Don't let your budget get in the way of enjoying life and trying something new. This is why it's key to stash away some money for when your new hobby inspiration strikes. As I've mentioned previously, you could try out Acorns or Tip Yourself to get your fund started. Maybe use your profits from Chapter 8 (Making Extra Money) on your new hobby or simply create a line-item in your budget for "Rainy Day Fund" and contribute a little each month.

> **Frankie's Finer Points**: There are tons of hobbies you can try that cost little or no money: reading, writing, hiking, cycling, cooking, and baking, for starters. There are also hobbies you can try that might *make* you some extra money when you sell your goods: think candle making, roasting coffee, and knitting dog sweaters.

63 INVEST IN YOUR FRIENDSHIPS.

While staying connected with friends is a good human thing to do in general, it can also lead to unexpected benefits during your financial journey. Friendship means always being there for one another, and this can even translate to your finances. How? Find a financial accountability partner. Make sure to choose someone you trust completely, and I recommend that they have a similar financial situation as yourself if possible. While you're going through so many big financial changes, it's important to not only lean on your friend for support but to celebrate the wins – and do the same for them! Be sure to check in on a regular basis and offer each other support and advice, because managing your money can be hard enough on our own!

> **Frankie's Finer Points**: Become the "social director" within your friend group. Instead of always going out for dinner, drinks, or brunch, organize some fun and budget-friendly events that you all will enjoy. Every year I host a "blind wine" tasting event and I'll also often invite friends over for football viewing parties (and yes, even The Bachelor…). When guests ask what to bring I'll give specific requests so we've got a variety of

dishes and aren't tempted to order in. Other inexpensive friend activities include going for a group hike with a picnic finish, throwing a cookie decorating competition, or even a nice dose of nostalgia by trying out the local bowling alley with a discounted group rate!

11

TRAVEL

Guess what: you can pay off your debt, save money, and still take a vacation without feeling guilty. Travel has always been very important to me and I certainly wasn't willing to give it up completely in the pursuit of my financial goals. In fact, I spent over 40 days in 2018 traveling, half of which was international. Making this work with my budget just took a little flexibility, a lot of planning, and a mission-driven attitude.

64 TAKE A ROAD TRIP.

But not spontaneously on a Friday night. Put it on your calendar a few months out and plan it thoughtfully so you're not breaking the bank by being underprepared (e.g. pack snacks, borrow equipment, ask a neighbor to watch your cats, go with friends and split gas). Personally, I need that "light at the end of the 5-day-work-week-grind tunnel" to look forward to, and a road trip is just the ticket. Odds are, there are lots of great places within a two or three-hour drive that you've never stopped to check out. Get out for a weekend and scratch that wanderlust itch on the cheap!

In my neck of the woods, it's especially fun (and extremely affordable) to go camping. Add in a hike for some fresh air and free exercise. If you have a 9 to 5 and are able, take off Friday or Monday (I personally vote Monday) and make it a 3-day weekend. The extra day can help you avoid traffic and allow yourself to free your mind up and really enjoy your time away. Enjoy the change of scenery, enjoy your loved ones (or alone time!), disconnect from technology, but mostly just… relax. There's something to be said for a little time off to refresh and re-energize, no matter how short!

65 FIND A WAY TO LODGE FOR FREE.

Have a second uncle twice removed that's always talking about their beach house during family reunions? Maybe a friend has an Airbnb or owns a campsite that often sits unoccupied. Don't feel guilty: ask to use their place for a little getaway. I've come to learn that vacation homeowners WANT to share their space with others. That's half the reason they bought it in the first place. Plus, it might help you reconnect with that distant relative or high school friend that you lost touch with!

Here are a few more simple ways to "get away" for a night or two:

- Camp out in a friend's backyard
- Bring your significant other on a work trip and stay an extra day or two
- Offer to house sit for a friend going out of town

Frankie's Finer Points: If you know someone in a different state or country, set up a house-swap. You'll both get to stay somewhere new for free, plus you have the added benefit of someone watching your house while you're on vacation!

66 BE FLEXIBLE ABOUT YOUR TRAVEL DATES AND AIRPORT LOCATIONS.

By far the easiest way to save money on traveling is to be flexible with where and when you're going. Instead of paying top dollar to fly to Paris for the week of Christmas ($$$), use one of the many travel websites like Travelzoo to help you find an awesome and inexpensive location that you might not have even considered before. Sometimes the most fun part of traveling is just spinning a globe and seeing where your next vacation will be – this is like the budget-friendly version of that!

If you definitely have a destination in mind, then travel on off-days (use Smart Travel's guide of The Best and Worst Days to Fly) and include the "nearby airports" filter in your flight searches. Use websites like KAYAK and Skyscanner to set up low fare alerts. Use your mileage points, and even buy points if you're super close to a key threshold that will save you money. Just don't ever accept the first rates you find. Chances are, there are deals out there you can find now but even better deals if you're willing to be patient, flexible, and put in some time doing research.

> **Frankie's Finer Points**: Another incredible site I regularly use and highly recommend is Google Flights. Google is the best search engine for the internet after all! You can set up alerts easily and see the cheapest flights by date and location using a visual map. When you find a great deal that you want to book, I suggest purchasing directly on the airline's website. You'll almost always find the same price as Google Flights, but if you need to make any modifications to your flight, it's much easier to work directly with the airline

67 MAXIMIZE AND USE CREDIT CARD POINTS

I've touched on this in the Credit Card chapter, but I'll reiterate here that you need to make sure you fully understand the benefits of your credit card(s). If you've opted for a card with travel rewards, make sure you really understand the ins and outs of how you can effectively rack up points, so you're maximizing your reward potential. For example, some cards will give you 2x, or even 4x, the rewards for using your card on purchases related to transportation or for booking airlines. So, before you pay for that Uber, take a second to make sure you're using the right card.

And, although it can be fun to see how many rewards points you can acquire, you signed up for that travel rewards credit card for a reason: Use. Those. Points! When you take that next trip, don't forget to use your points on those necessary travel-related expenses, like transportation from the airport to your hotel. It's little expenses like this that can really add up when traveling – but lucky you, with your hard-earned points, it's can be free!

68 ENJOY CREDIT CARD PERKS LIKE FREE LOUNGE ACCESS.

There are some great travel perks out there: flight cancellation reimbursement, covering rental car insurance, free TSA PreCheck, and more. My personal favorite? Free lounge access at the airport. Lounges will afford you free snacks and drinks (even alcohol), comfy and spacious seating, TVs, free WiFi, charging stations, and guaranteed celebrity run-ins. Kidding about that last one but we did see Jack White in a lounge in New York!

If you're the kind of person that likes to get to the airport *extremely* early or if you simply get stuck on an aggressively long layover, pay for lounge access and try it out for yourself. At the end of the day, this can actually make good financial sense if you would be otherwise sitting in a sad airport restaurant or bar racking up a similar tab.

My favorite travel credit card is Chase Ultimate Rewards. Along with the $300 in travel credits and free Global Entry, the perks include free access to the Priority Pass network of airport lounges. Use the Priority Pass website to see where all the lounges are located and be sure to read the exclusions and hours carefully. After a long flight, I once trekked to the exact opposite side of an airport for a lounge only to find out my Priority Pass membership wasn't accepted after 9:00 pm. With Chase's Priority Pass membership, you can even bring up to two guests with you for free. If you have a fourth, individuals tend to cost $50 or less. Split that four ways and you're looking at a cool $12.50 or less per person for an awesome airport experience – how often can you say that?! With the amount of food and drinks you all are bound to consume, it's well worth it. Not to mention using a clean, private bathroom...

One of my favorite trips of 2018 was the shortest: from Seattle to central Oregon. There were four of us traveling and I was excited to share my lounge experience with the group. I could feel the group's nervous energy as I navigated the extra guest, and they seemed surprised when we got through to the private lounge without an issue. While it probably looked like I had paid someone handsomely under the table for the celebrity treatment, it's just a simple travel hack most people don't know about!

69 BOOK ACTIVITIES ON YOUR VACATION FOR CHEAP.

As I've mentioned before, you should thoroughly explore your credit card's rewards portal. I was surprised to stumble upon an "activities" section for my credit card and even more surprised to find that some activities only cost 1,000 to 2,000 points, equivalent to 15 to 30 bucks! When my girlfriend and I took our Europe trip, we booked wine and cheese tasting, a murder mystery walking tour, a Thames River cruise with included brunch, and more all for *free* via my credit card rewards.

Another great way to find "experiences" is Airbnb. Not only do they have lodging options, but you can also go on experiences with a local host. Generally, these experiences are very affordable and take up hours of time you might otherwise devote to eating tourism-inflated food or buying expensive show tickets.

One of our absolute favorite experiences in Paris was booked through Airbnb. With a small group, we met with a local celebrity chef, drank espresso together, explored a local market, shopped for fresh fruits and vegetables, and then went to her home to cook and eat an authentic Parisian meal. One of the first things we did when we got home was explore Airbnb experiences locally in Seattle!

70 FIND BUDGET-FRIENDLY PET AND HOUSE SITTERS.

Ask a friend or neighbor to sit your pets, water your plants, or check in on your home every couple of days. People generally are happy to help, especially knowing that you would return the favor next time they're out of town. Don't forget to give them a thank you: a plate of cookies, a bottle of wine, or even money (a reasonable amount). Going with a friend is far cheaper (and safer) than sites like Wag! or Rover. And it's definitely less stressful leaving your belongings and pet(s) with someone you know and trust. Whenever I go out of town, my brother will watch my dog Tucker (in exchange for ample amounts of double-chocolate brownies, of course) and he always texts me pictures and updates so I know he's in good hands and having fun.

71 DON'T GET STUCK PAYING INTERNATIONAL FEES.

Don't get stuck paying foreign exchange fees or cell phone roaming fees. Make sure to always contact your banks and credit card company before you travel so you understand any fees they might have that you can avoid and also so you don't get locked out of your accounts. Also, contact your cell phone provider and see what travel options they provide. Some companies will charge a flat fee per day when abroad, some charge fees a week at a time, and some might not have fees but will throttle your data usage. It took me a cool 10 minutes to find the information I needed from my providers, and I saved a ton of money and headaches by coordinating in advance.

12

NAVIGATING HOLIDAYS & SPECIAL OCCASIONS

I'm including this section because #1 – the holidays can be a very difficult time of the year to continue good habits and not "undo" months of progress you've already made and #2 – you can get great at budgeting for bills and working towards financial goals all you want, but remembering to set money aside for special events and gifts is something a lot of us struggle with. Here are some quick and dirty tips this holiday season and beyond:

72 CHANGE THE WAY YOU EXCHANGE GIFTS.

This tip requires buy-in from your friends and family. If your loved ones are onboard, consider ending (or seriously reducing) your gift giving. Instead of buying each other gifts for every major holiday, anniversary, and birthday, treat each other to home-cooked meals and quality time spent together. If you NEED to scratch that gift-giving itch, try agreeing on just one gift-exchange occasion each year. You and your loved ones might find you appreciate the extra cash and the reduced stress of shopping for gifts – a gift in and of itself! If gift giving is too big of a tradition to give up, here are other ideas to reduce the expenses:

- Instead of exchanging presents with everyone in your family and/or friends group, try out a Secret Santa or White Elephant. This can be a really fun and silly way to spend time with your loved ones, and it won't break anybody's bank.

- Have a significant other or best friend that you swap gifts with? Do you find you both outdo the last year by 5%, 10% or more? Set an honest budget this time, at least 10% *below* last year. OR, simply agree to put a set amount of money into a shared "vacation" fund for gift-giving holidays. See how this goes for a year and revisit the conversation next year – nothing has to be permanent!

- Any 30 Rock fans out there? For one holiday episode, Jack and Liz agree to exchange "zero dollar" gifts and see who can be the most thoughtful. Liz ends up calling in a bomb threat to Penn Station so that Jack's girlfriend misses her train and they get to spend more time together. Don't EVER do that... but try out some mutual "zero dollar" gifting with your friends and see what creative ideas you come up with!

- If you can, gift something you have access to for free through your work. Many years ago, my best friend gave me a t-shirt his wife likely got for free or cheap through her job. I still wear it several times a month, and love it! Another friend gifts coffee from the local roastery she works at. One of my favorite gifts annually is the calendar my brother gets from his company. Point is, you don't have to spend money to be a good gift giver! Good friends won't care if their gift was cheap or free.

But keep buying gifts for the kids if you have any in your close circle. It's still all about them...

73 IF YOU MUST GIFT, SCORE THE BEST DEAL.

Whenever possible, plan your gifting well in advance so you can score the best deals. Shop using sites like Brad's Deals, which list all the online coupon codes and best store discounts for you, hand-picked by the staff. If you have a specific gift in mind, set up alerts using deal sites like Craigslist, Amazon, and even apps like BuyVia and Yroo and wait for the item to go on sale.

Another reason to plan so far ahead? So you can budget and pay in full. Here's a quick lesson I learned the hard way: if you're in credit card debt and paying 20% interest on your balance and you buy something on sale using credit... you're no longer buying that item on sale. In some cases, it may end up costing you more than the retail value due to interest accrued over time.

74 DON'T SHOP DURING CYBER WEEK OR PRIME DAY.

On Black Friday, Cyber Monday, and Prime Day, it's not financially smart to casually browse and see what's out there; you'll end up making so many unplanned and unnecessary purchases solely because they were on sale.

The only way to avoid major spending is to plan way ahead. Think beyond Christmas gifts. Make a list throughout the year of big-ticket items that you actually want for yourself or for others (e.g. a KitchenAid mixer, a Roomba, a new TV) and then ONLY shop the cyber deals if those specific items are on sale. If you use Cyber Week for holiday gifts, keep in mind that these days, you might find the same products at even BETTER deals in the weeks leading up to Christmas, Hanukkah, and Kwanzaa. Sometimes it pays to procrastinate!

Frankie's Finer Points: Don't forget to keep an eye on prices AFTER you buy so you can get a price adjustment if the price goes down within your return window (I'm looking at you, Best Buy KitchenAid 5 quart mixer).

75 RETHINK THE HOLIDAY DECORATIONS.

Outdoor lights, blow-up lawn decorations, decked trees, cozy candles, gingerbread houses, nutcrackers, fake snow, ugly sweaters, pine wreaths abound... It can certainly be fun to participate in festive holiday decor but consider toning it down this year. Yes, it's fun to pick out your own tree and chop it down, but it's also expensive – the average tree will set you back $50. Year after year, that's hundreds of dollars that could be better spent invested (with compounding interest!).

Maybe this is the year that you invest in an artificial tree from Target during the off-season! Or, maybe this is the year that you cut out some paper snowflakes with your friends and call it good. Think of new, thrifty traditions that will keep you on track with your goals *and* spread that holiday cheer.

76 MAKE YOUR HALLOWEEN COSTUME THIS YEAR.

Don't forget, December isn't the only month that can get expensive for holidays. It's easy to get carried away on Halloween to try to win the award for best costume. Has this scenario happened to you?: Looks at the calendar. Sees it's October 29th. Forgot to plan ahead. Goes online and rush orders a way-too-expensive costume because it's last second. Goes to party and 10 other people are wearing the same costume.

Plan ahead and *make* your costume this year! Or better yet, take a year off from Halloween altogether... but maybe that's just the Grinch in me. Either way, don't attend that exclusive dance party downtown or hit up all the bars – and then top it all off with a 3x surge price Uber ride home and a nasty hangover. Host a B.Y.O.B. house party while dressed as Sandy or Danny – that requires a wig at most (and maybe an awesome leather jacket that you're secretly super excited to wear year round)! My girlfriend and I did this couples costume last year and we were shocked at how popular it was.

13

EDUCATION (AKA MY TOP TENS)

The following tools come as a personal recommendation after spending a year of sifting through all of my financial clutter. This chapter could be easy to just skim and check off, but to really gain lasting life skills be sure your financial education is ongoing. Personally, I didn't set rules for myself around learning more about money, but you might want to (e.g. devote an hour a day to financial podcasts). But, if you're like me, once you get started you might find that learning about your finances is fun and not a chore, especially with my favorite picks from the year!

77 READ AT LEAST TWO OF THESE BOOKS COVER TO COVER.

Reading is good for the soul. It's a screen-free way to pass a spare moment or unwind after work while increasing your imagination, vocabulary, and overall smarts. There's truly no downside to reading; if you can think of one, shoot me a message. It's easier than ever to take a book on the go these days with eBooks. I enjoy reading while taking public transportation, on a lunch break, and especially before bed.

As I mentioned earlier, it can be a totally free hobby if you utilize the library, or you can find free downloads of many books on apps like Kindle.

Here are my top ten personal finance reads I discovered in 2018:

1. The Money Resolution
What do you know... you're already reading that one!

2. Rich Dad Poor Dad
The ultimate starting point for eye-opening financial education in my opinion

3. The Total Money Makeover
Dave Ramsey is considered by many to be the king of personal finance

4. Meet The Frugalwoods
Half novel, half frugal advice, all page-turning and relatable

5. The Automatic Millionaire
A quick read with powerful lessons around compound interest

6. The Financial Diet
A beginners guide like mine with a bigger focus on budget tracking, interviews, and charts

7. You Are A Badass At Making Money
Personable and uplifting – a great audiobook listen

8. The 4-Hour Workweek
How to be efficient with your time and work life so you can focus on the things that matter

9. The Millionaire Next Door
Analyzes the psychology behind spending patterns spanning many decades

10. The Simple Path To Wealth
A straightforward and simple approach to all things personal finance. A fun and easy read!

78 SUBSCRIBE TO AT LEAST THREE OF THESE (PERSONAL FINANCE) PODCASTS.

Podcasts are super in right now and ostensibly here to stay. You might have heard it's the golden era for podcasts and it's true. Some are even becoming hit tv shows! So if you haven't tuned in to a podcast since Serial, you have some catching up to do!

You can use the stock podcast app on your phone but I also recommend Stitcher and Overcast. With these apps, you can automatically download the latest episodes so they're always handy and won't use valuable cell phone data or drop on the subway. These are my favorite money podcasts that I subscribe to:

1. Stacking Benjamins
My personal go-to on Monday, Wednesday and Friday. Lighthearted and fun with great guests, trivia, listener questions, and roundtable discussions.

2. Money in the Morning
Posted first on Facebook Live, this podcast usually covers one to two recent stories with live fan interaction

3. How to Money AND Listen Money Matters
Beer plus money talk. Need I say more? These two podcasts are extremely similar and both are a hoot

4. The Side Hustle Show
Posted frequently and each episode includes a 45-minute interview with a side hustler

5. So Money
Host Farnoosh Torabi has very candid conversations with some of the brightest minds in business and personal finance

6. The Smart Passive Income Podcast
Self-described as "working hard now, so you can sit back and reap the benefits later" – very inspirational listen for those looking towards early retirement

7. The Mad Fientist
Thought-provoking conversations with individuals that have reached financial independence, each in their own unique way

8. Debt Free in 30
Practical advice on personal finance, delivered in a quick 30-minute episode

9. Bad With Money
Host Gaby Dunn, who's 2019 book Bad With Money: The Imperfect Art of Getting your Financial Sh** Together is next on my reading list, is hilarious and make finances... fun!

10. Afford Anything
This podcast is based on the idea that "you can afford anything, but you can't afford everything"

Others you might enjoy: Listen Money Matters, Her Money Matters, Motley Fool Money, Planet Money... it's becoming apparent that I'm *obsessed* with financial podcasts. How could I not be? They're so easy to enjoy: I put these on when walking the dog, doing the dishes, working out (nothing pumps me up more!), on a road trip, or even taking a shower.

> **Even Frankie's Finer Points**: Set your playback speed to 1.25X or even 1.5X. This makes getting through episodes so much more efficient!

79 FREQUENT AT LEAST FOUR OF THESE PERSONAL FINANCE SITES.

All of the websites are constantly churning content about everything personal finance. Save at least four of these blogs and websites in your browser's "favorites" folder and check in on them often, ideally at least once a week:

1. The Points Guy (www.thepointsguy.com)

2. Magnify Money (www.magnifymoney.com)

3. NerdWallet (www.nerdwallet.com)

4. Kiplinger (www.kiplinger.com)

5. The Simple Dollar (www.thesimpledollar.com)

6. Good Financial Cents (www.goodfinancialcents.com)

7. The Penny Hoarder (www.thepennyhoarder.com)

8. Mr. Money Mustache (www.mrmoneymustache.com)

9. Cait Flanders (www.caitflanders.com)

10. And of course, the **r/personalfinance** sub on Reddit (www.reddit.com/r/personalfinance)

> **Frankie's Finer Points**: I also highly recommend Google News. After exploring many of the websites above, it learns my preferences and tailors my news content based on my interests. By now, about half of my feed on any given day is articles about personal finance.

80 USE AT LEAST FIVE FINANCIAL APPS ON A REGULAR BASIS.

Five financial apps might sound like a lot, but I'll give you two freebies: your mobile banking app and your credit card app. Beyond those, download a few more from the list below and check them out regularly. Some of these apps will help you save money, some make micro investments, and some help provide easy-to-digest information:

1. Acorns
Rounds up your purchases and invests the extra change

2. Betterment and/or Wealthfront
Robo-investing at its best, these apps are very similar and seemingly offering more and more services every month

3. Robinhood
Easy, commission-free trading

4. Stockpile
Buy partial stocks of brands you love – an excellent first look into the market for stock-buying rookies

5. M1 Finance

An intuitive investing app that doesn't charge commission or platform fees. It allows fractional share purchasing and auto-investments.

6. Twine

Great way to save money with a partner – this app can pull money from two separate bank accounts to invest or save towards shared goals

7. Tip Yourself

Kick yourself cash whenever you'd like, for whatever you'd like

8. Mint and/or Clarity Money

Helps you track and organize your spending habits, upcoming bills, goal progress, and much more

9. Qapital

Another automated savings app like Acorns. Excellent for freelancers as it even has a great option for automatically saving a percentage of each paycheck for taxes

10. Digit

Once connected to a bank account of your choosing, Digit monitors your spending patterns and automatically moves money into a rainy day fund. It will also occasionally text you silly GIFs...

Plus, there is new "FinTech" (financial technology) popping up almost everyday so be sure to keep your eye on the App Store if you have a specific need in mind.

81 WATCH THESE TEN YOUTUBE VIDEOS.

YouTube is great because lots of videos are packed into just 5 to 10 minutes and easy to digest on the fly. Plus, it's available on most devices and even comes as a stock app on most new smart TVs. It's a great resource for watching reviews of sites and apps that you're considering, or to help you learn about specific financial topics that you're struggling with. And much like the Google News app I recommended earlier, YouTube learns your interests and ensures your feed is full of video recommendations that you'll love! That autoplay feature at the end of each video can honestly keep me hooked for an hour or more like I'm binging something wonderful on Netflix!

Here are my top 10 videos that I recommend you watch. The whole list shouldn't take you more than the time it takes to watch one feature-length film. Check them out:

1. How to Invest $1,000 for 2018 | Wealth Hacker - Jeff Rose

2. 9 Money Truths I Wish I Knew Sooner | The Financial Diet

3. The Minimalist Approach To Personal Finance |Matt D'Avella

4. Ask Ramit: 401k's, Roth IRA, & the Ladder of Personal Finance | I Will Teach You To Be Rich

5. Tony Robbins 7 Simple Steps to Financial Freedom | Lewis Howes

6. All the financial advice you'll ever need fits on a single index card | PBS NewsHour

7. Why the Rich are Getting Richer | Robert Kiyosaki | TEDxUCSD

8. How to Properly Manage Your Money Like the Rich | Tom Ferry

9. The 5 BEST Credit Cards for Beginners (2019) | Graham Stevens

10. How To Invest in 2019 (How ANYONE can be RICH) | Graham Stevens

Bonus: And just because it's incredibly adorable: We Gave Kids One Hour To Spend $100 by BuzzFeedVideo

Pop Quiz!

1. The best place to obtain books is called the _____. *Hint: It rhymes with Liar Barry*

2. I recommend you listen to podcasts at what speed?
    A. 0.25x
    B. 1.25x
    C. 1,000x
    D. Normal speed while sleeping with headphones on because of the power of osmosis

3. What app did I use to document my journey? *Hint: I'm only hungry for retirement!*
    A. Apple Notes
    B. Eat24

C. Uber Eats

D. Postmates

4. Which site do I use to track my Net Worth?

A. Goodment

B. Betterment

C. Bestment

D. Worsement

Answers: 1) Library, 2) B, 3) A, 4) B

14

TEN SIMPLE THINGS YOU CAN DO RIGHT NOW

You've gotten this far. You're learning. You're motivated. But maybe... it's starting to feel a little overwhelming. I totally understand. This is almost a year's worth of my learnings and tips jam packed into 13 chapters so far. Let's take a step back. Let's achieve a couple quick wins – like, TODAY.

82 DELETE TEMPTING APPS AND SAVED WEBSITES.

Go ahead and delete shopping apps like Groupon, Living Social, Zappos, Etsy, Amazon, and especially Prime Now if you have access to that in your area. If you really want to use these apps, you'll have to log onto a computer. That might be enough of a deterrent to help curb the cravings.

It's the same concept for time-sucking apps like Facebook and Instagram – time is money! Taking them off your phone can seriously reduce the time you spend wasting time. Instead, download some financial independence podcasts and videos, and stay on your goals. (Okay... maybe keep Instagram. It's designed for mobile and we all love the Gram. But monitor your usage if your phone has that feature!)

Personally, I also deleted a few of my saved "things to do around town" sites from my bookmarks. Sure, I might miss out on the "Harry Potter Improv Performance Turned Musical" at the local dive bar... but that's okay. I can miss a few of those a year.

83 CLAIM FREE CASH.

Who doesn't like free money? See if you're eligible to claim some cash via this Today Show article titled "Are you owed money? Here's how to find out — without getting scammed![15]" There are more sites out there, organized by state, that can tell you if you're owed money, too – just make sure it's from a reputable source because there are some copycat scammers out there. These sites might tell you that you're part of a class action refund or you're due an insurance claim check, for example. While you're at it, also check your Venmo, PayPal, Google Pay, and other cash app balances. You might be surprised; it's like finding a five dollar bill in your pants after doing the wash. While you're at it... go through all your pant pockets and couch cushions!

84 HAVE A SPEND-FREE DAY.

There are days when you end up not spending money on anything, and I'm betting you survived. Now, try doing this purposefully. Not only will you save money, but this exercise can help you detox from your consumer "gotta have it now" mindset. Make your own coffee and take it to work, pack a lunch, invite friends over for a happy hour at your house, kick back and watch a new release from the library, or take your dog for a long walk in the park – all without spending any money.

Commit to going an entire day without spending any money using cash or cards. This'll be easy, so next challenge yourself to a week. No problem? Try it for a month! It should go without mentioning but this isn't an excuse to not pay your bills...

85 ADJUST YOUR GOALS.

Goals aren't always something that you should set and forget: you might reach milestones slower or faster than you anticipated, or you might find that your goals grow and morph as your journey progresses or your life situation changes. What you initially thought was a priority might not be as urgent a few months down the road. And that's okay.

Adjusting your goals is something you should consider doing several times a year. If you haven't brainstormed any goals yet, stop and do that today. As I've said before, what I look for in a goal is *challenging*, *measurable*, and *achievable*, but that's not a requirement. Some people might preach making hard and fast rules around goal setting and tracking. I say your goals should be whatever is going to keep YOU motivated every day.

86 TRY A NEW (CHEAPER) WAY TO GET TO WORK.

Do you drive yourself to work? Are you paying ridiculous amounts (aka anything) for parking? Try biking tomorrow. Take public transportation the next day. See if you can coordinate a carpool, and split gas money. Try out Waze Carpool or Scoop. If your work has a subsidized or even free bus pass, USE IT. If work allows you to put aside pre-tax money towards transportation – set that up!

For me, it was super easy to find my bus pass form through my work's HR intranet portal. Printing it off was easy. Filling it out, a cinch. Taking 2 minutes out of my day to walk it down a hall to a human... now that was nearly impossible. But just do it already! Wow, that might be the most millennial thing I've admitted to yet...

87 DONATE YOUR MONEY OR YOUR TIME.

As you grow through this financial journey, it's important to not become a money-hoarding scrooge, rolling around in piles of cash as you laugh maniacally to yourself. As you build wealth, try to budget a little extra (honestly, as small as $5 a month) for others – it'll feel great, and a little good karma never hurt anyone.

There are so many easy ways to donate: from dropping off goods and clothes to Goodwill, to setting up a recurring $20 monthly donation to a charity that means a lot to you. If you're at a place financially where you can't spare any extra dough, try to spend a few hours a month donating your time. Read to children at your local library, pass out meals at the food bank, or work a booth at a local fundraising event.

In August of 2018, I did something incredibly meaningful that made me feel far more fulfilled than any money I made or invested. I rode in Obliteride, a bike event sponsored by Fred Hutchinson Cancer Research Center, after raising $914 for cancer research with family, friend, and work donations. I also supported my niece's dance team last year with cash contributions and by participating in a more-intense-than-anticipated team Bunco night and silent auction. I have zero regrets about spending a little time and money on these causes. If anything, I regret not doing more sooner.

Write off donations on your taxes if you want, but either way, philanthropy is a good reminder that, while you're working on yourself, there are always people out there that are less fortunate. We can *all* afford to give a little.

88 BE SMART WITH YOUR CASH.

There are two camps for cash: some people find cash-only to be a very useful way to budget (e.g. "the envelope system"), while others come across cash and all budgetary rules fly out the window. Personally, I'm in that second group. When I have cash, I can literally feel it burning a hole in my pocket and I'll spend it on the first thing I see. For me, it's really usefully to take any cash I have (yes, even if it's just $5) and deposit it directly into my savings account. This has been a hugely beneficial habit for me, and really curbed splurges. Plus, knowing myself and how I treat cash, I usually request Venmo even when others are trying to reimburse me or pay me with cash.

89 RETURN A GIFT OR SELL A GIFT CARD.

That gift you got from your grandma that you don't like? Chances are, it came with tags on and maybe even a receipt. Return it and buy something you actually love, or heck, take the cash and put it in your rainy day fund. She'd want it that way... That gift card you've had in your wallet for months (or maybe years)? Sell it online, less 10-20% – you'll come out with some easy, free cash!

A personal anecdote: For my birthday one year, I asked my mom for a gift card to the Apple Store to put towards a new phone I desperately needed. I unwrapped my gift and *gasp* in front of me were five $20 gift cards for iTunes. Close mom, but not quite. Being the good son that I am, I hugged her and told her I loved it. Two days later, I sold the lot for $80 on Craigslist. I had 10 hits in one hour after posting a quick ad. Mom, if you're reading this... sorry! And thank you for the $80 that did go towards my new phone!

90 SIGN UP FOR (A FEW) PROMOTIONAL EMAILS & UNSUBSCRIBE FROM OTHERS.

It's not all spam! If you can trust yourself to be responsible and not go on a shopping spree, sign up for email updates for the places that you truly shop often. If you'd be shopping there either way, you'll likely come out ahead with great deals and special offers. Use a backup email address if you'd rather keep this kind of email out of your main inbox and further from temptation. Again, only sign up for promotional emails for stores you'd frequent either way.

While you're doing this, also take the time to go through your inbox and declutter. Unsubscribe from the emails that aren't functional and only tempt you to buy junk, and *don't* look back. You won't miss three emails a day from [insert Silly Cat Store on Etsy you purchased from five years ago].

Just a few weeks ago, I was in line at H&M to buy a shirt. It was a long line so I went on their website and in a matter of seconds I signed up for email alerts and earned 20% off that purchase that day, right then and there. No questions asked!

91 ASSIGN YOUR BENEFICIARIES.

This isn't very fun to think about, but it's an absolute must. For your bank accounts, investments, life insurance policy, house deed (if you're so lucky), etc. – take 30 minutes today and designate who the beneficiary will be in case something happens to you. Be sure you're taking care of your loved ones and thinking ahead, especially as you add new accounts and gain more wealth. Even if you're certain you've done this, go through them all, double check, and adjust if necessary.

15

GENERAL DOS (AND DON'TS!)

"Life is 10% what you make it and 90% how you take it." - *Irving Berlin*

Are you the kind of person who just needs some hard and fast rules to follow? Look no further. Here are useful Dos and Don'ts when it comes to personal finance. As I've mentioned before, there are lots of ways to tackle several of these steps. It's up to you to determine how to approach most of these based on your goals and life situation.

92 DO TALK ABOUT MONEY.

Talk about money with your family, with your friends, and especially with your significant other. Talk about money with your coworkers and with strangers you meet on the street. Money should NOT be a taboo subject. You can learn. You can share. You have nothing to be ashamed of. We're all fighting this battle and it's very likely many of us are struggling with the same things. Or, even better, by talking openly about financial hardships we might all be able to help each other!

93 DON'T COMPARE YOURSELF TO OTHERS.

There will always be someone who is more successful than you, but also there will always be someone worse off than you. Everyone is different. Everyone has different lifestyles and goals. It benefits no one to compare yourself to others, so try to stay away from that noise. Just keep moving forward in your own personal journey, and learning from your victories and mistakes, one step and one day at a time.

94 DO SET A PLAN (INCLUDING GOALS) WITH YOUR PARTNER.

It's commonly cited that finances are one of the leading causes of divorce. If you don't communicate, work together, and set common goals with your partner, it's pretty likely that your relationship will fall apart… sorry to be the bearer of bad news. My girlfriend and I have a financial situation that works extremely well for us, but please make sure to talk with your partner about what your best plan of action is. Here's what we do:

I pay for all of our shared expenses on one card (works great for me, I'm playing the credit cards points game!), add it up, and then we split it 60/40 – a ratio we came up with based on income. These costs are things like groceries, travel expenses, transportation, and date nights. My girlfriend also pays her portion of the rent on the 1st and a flat amount for bills on the 15th, based on our 60/40 model outlined above. Finding the fair amount for utilities took some work since that bill fluctuates, but I only had to sit down once for about 20 minutes to figure out our monthly average over a six month period and then split it up. And although this bill does change monthly, it's not worth nickel-and-diming each other to figure it out exactly. Bill fluctuations even out in the wash at the end of the year. Again, we're both paying a fair amount – and I get all the credit card points! This is obviously a personal situation. Have an open and honest conversation with your partner to determine a plan that works for both of you.

Frankie's Finer Points: Set a weekly or monthly meeting to go over your finances. Make sure you're each on target to meet your goals, talk about what you've been struggling with, and celebrate your victories. You COULD make it just a quick 15-30 minute check-in... OR... *drum roll* make it a fun date night that you look forward to by adding wine and cheese or having it during happy hour at a local pub. Who knew you could look forward to a meeting about finances?!

95 DON'T BECOME OBSESSED WITH PERSONAL FINANCES.

It's a marathon, not a sprint. You don't have to make 101 lifestyle changes all at once. Map them out. Set a plan. Take it step by step. Skip some of these steps. Add some steps of your own. Change my challenge to a two-year plan. It's your life and there is no "one size fits all" plan. Money isn't everything so don't let yourself become so obsessed that you don't allow yourself to enjoy life. Rome wasn't built in a day, and neither is your retirement portfolio.

96 DO FILE YOUR TAXES EARLY.

Death and taxes – we all know the line. Yes, taxes are the worst and can be extremely stressful but do yourself a favor and get them out of the way this year. Avoid late fees, and give yourself time to budget if you need to cough up some money to Uncle Sam. And if you're owed a refund, even better! You can use that money as a springboard to start your emergency fund or an investment portfolio.

This year, try to file your taxes on your own or for cheap or even free. After years of scheduling expensive appointments with tax accountants, I finally tried filing online with H&R Block. It was less than $40 and much easier than anticipated.

97 DON'T PLAY THE LOTTERY.

Never count on any form of the lottery as your get-rich-quick scheme. Apparently, odds are greater that you'll get hit by a meteorite than win the Big One and you're fives times more likely to get hit by lightning – twice. If you really want to satisfy that old gambling itch, I'd recommend a cheap scratch ticket instead of a lottery ticket. No, the winnings aren't as high, but frankly, you're not going to win the Big One anyways. The reason I would endorse a scratcher over a lottery ticket is that some of them can take a good 15 minutes to complete. For $2-5, it can be a pretty fun and cheap entertainment option! My favorites are the crossword and bingo scratchers. That said… it's probably best to not waste your money! But, you do you.

Frankie's Finer Points: Always get your tickets scanned, even if you're certain it's a loser. I kept a (small) pile of losers throughout the year and had them all checked one day. I found out I had almost thrown away $12 in winners that I just missed!

98 DO AVOID LIFESTYLE CREEP.

Let me help you identify the creeps in your life (money creeps, I can't help you with the other ones...). First, what is lifestyle creep? Generally, as people earn more money or have more money in savings or even fall into a bonus or inheritance – they tend to start spending more. The things you used to be happy with (the small apartment, homemade lunches, and a 2008 Subaru) suddenly seem lame since you can now afford "better".

So, often unconsciously, your lifestyle starts creeping towards more expensive likes to keep pace with your increased earnings. Rather than continue to live a modest lifestyle and put the extra money in savings and investments, you find yourself needing more and more money to keep up with your changing lifestyle (and maybe even the Joneses next door). This especially happens to young adults fresh out of school, when they land their first "grown-up" job and can suddenly afford nicer things.

What are some examples of creeps to look out for? Creeps can be tricky to recognize because they are mostly psychological (as are most things money!). You convince yourself that buying more will make you happy, especially after years of being so good and avoiding any kind of splurge purchases. It's different for everyone but here are some personal examples of times when my lifestyle creeped:

- When I was 22, and a recent college graduate that moved for my teaching job, I flew back to Seattle to visit friends and family roughly once a month.
- Last year, I added the local sports package to my cable company bill when I got a raise because I just *had* to have Red Zone.
- Also last year, we squeezed in a vacation to Denver in July because we simply couldn't wait 10 whole months for our Europe trip. Because, you know, when

is the next time you'll hear Seal at Red Rocks?! (We don't even really like Seal…)

Avoid the creeps. Aim to consistently live below your means so that you can retire on time (or early!) and live a comfortable and debt-free life.

99 DO VISUALIZE YOUR SUCCESSES AND WRITE THEM DOWN.

It can be hard to see the "financial freedom light" at the end of the "forever debt tunnel." Trust me, I know. But it's absolutely critical you believe in yourself because, as with many things in life, attitude is everything.

So what does that look like? My favorite way to visualize your successes is to write a letter to your future self (try futureme.org/). Write to the person you visualize you'll become. Write your fears. Your excitement. Your goals. Remind your future self why you've decided to take this leap into your personal finances. Who is inspiring you? What is inspiring you? Describe where you see yourself one year from now and, hopefully, when future you opens the letter you'll be proud.

100 DO GET STARTED – AND CELEBRATE YOUR VICTORIES ALONG THE WAY!

Guess what. You already got started by reading this book! Take the next step by downloading and printing my checklist (at www.TheMoneyResolution.com or www.etsy.com/shop/The-MoneyResolution). Set your goals including one to try 80 of these steps this year – be sure to check them off just for trying, even if you didn't necessarily succeed! Post the checklist some-where where you'll see it every day.

Equally important is making sure to acknowledge your successes, however large or small, in a responsible way! Did you just save your first $1,000 ever? Take yourself out for that bacon maple bar you've been wanting to try. Did you just pay off all your credit card debt? By all means, use your travel points and take yourself on vacation! It's important to celebrate your victo-ries, it'll help you stay motivated. And you deserve it!

*PAY IT FORWARD

"As you grow older, you will discover that you have two hands, one for helping yourself, the other for helping others." - Audrey Hepburn

101 PAY IT FORWARD

*Sorry, but this chapter is mandatory – no skippin'!

My ultimate goal in writing this book isn't just to help **you** become a better **you** financially, it's to help **us** become a better **us**. Giving, sharing, and being open-minded are the only ways to get us there. And that's how I settled on my 2019 resolution and reason for writing this book: *pay it forward.*

Paying it forward doesn't just mean sharing your wealth or donating to a cause (we've tackled that one already). I want you to pay it forward with your time and wisdom. Take what you've learned and help someone else in any way you can. Volunteer. Fundraise. Listen. Educate. Share your knowledge. Share this book! Start difficult conversations. Schedule that weekly finance check-in with your significant other. Find your accountability partner. Become a financial teacher! And yes, even donate your money because it feels good. Give because karma generally comes back around in unexpected ways, at unexpected times. We'll only get better if we all work together. We are in this together and we are greater together than apart.

My 2018 resolution turned my life around radically. And as a former educator, I understand the value of sharing knowledge and collaborating. That's what motivated me to share everything I learned in this past year and encourage others to jump-start their own journey.

Admittedly, it was pretty scary to put my story out there and write a book, especially when I'm not an expert on the subject (yet) and I've never published anything as an author. I have a lot to learn but I know I'm just getting started. I hope you'll continue to follow me in my journey and continue to grow in your own.

I had no idea that tackling my debt and taking charge of my personal finances would also help me tackle a bucket list item of writing a book. I want to know what this checklist might help YOU accomplish. I want to know how you paid it forward. Share your stories (however small or large) with me at frankie@themoneyresolution.com and follow my blog at www.themoneyresolution.com.

Thank you for reading and always remember:
Small efforts, day in and day out

THE INDEX CARD

Dr. Harold Pollack, author of "The Index Card", became famous for keeping finances simple. He claimed that the best personal finance advice can fit on a 3-by-5 index card. While I can't agree that finances are this straightforward for everybody and all life situations, I do admit that his advice (discovered early in my journey last year) encouraged me to keep it simple and helped me focus in on the most impactful money moves I could make.

With that in mind, I reflected on my 101 steps and boiled it all down to 10 big ideas that I think will make the most impact on our future finances. So I leave you with the key takeaways from this book. The CliffsNotes, if you will.

The Money Resolution Index Card

1. Set your financial goals and revisit them frequently

2. Ask for a raise or get a new, better paying job

3. Find out your credit score and create a plan to improve

4. Get completely out of credit card debt using the snowball approach

5. Save 3 months worth of expenses into an easy-to-access emergency fund

6. Open up and max out a Roth annually (be sure it's invested)

7. Max out your 401(k). Start with a "match" and increase 1% monthly

8. Choose a HDHP. Max out your HSA (invest funds over $1,000)

9. Find a side hustle - active and/or passive income

10. Pay it forward with your time and/or your money

ABOUT THE AUTHOR

Frankie grew up in Tacoma, WA and is a proud Stadium High School alum. He earned his B.A. in Communication from the University of Washington in 2007. Upon graduation, he taught high school English, drama, and film studies at San Jose High School for 4 years through Teach For America where he also directed an original play and musical, and coached the varsity baseball team. He went on to earn his Master of Education from the University of Washington in 2012. He's a proud triple-uncle, double-Husky, and single-father of Tucker the border collie. He blew the first ever paycheck he earned from Target at age 16 on a PlayStation 2 (#NoRegrets). He currently works as a Marketing Manager and lives in the Fremont neighborhood of Seattle, often daydreaming of the Seattle Supersonics returning. This is his first book, and one of several in the series he has planned.

REFERENCES

1 https://www.bankrate.com/personal-finance/smart-money/americans-and-financial-apps-survey-0218/

2 https://www.usinflationcalculator.com/inflation/current-inflation-rates/

3 https://www.nerdwallet.com/blog/banking/nerdwallets-best-cd-rates/

4 https://www.cnbc.com/2018/01/18/few-americans-have-enough-savings-to-cover-a-1000-emergency.html

5 https://www.fool.com/investing/2017/11/13/a-foolish-take-heres-how-much-debt-the-average-us.aspx

6 https://www.debt.org/faqs/americans-in-debt/demographics/

7 https://thepointsguy.com/guide/key-considerations-improving-credit-score/

8 https://www.nerdwallet.com/best/credit-cards/balance-transfer

9 https://www.daveramsey.com/blog/how-teens-can-become-millionaires

10 https://www.jhsph.edu/research/centers-and-institutes/johns-hopkins-center-for-a-livable-future/_pdf/research/clf_reports/importance-of-reducing-animal-product-consumption-and-wasted-food-in-mitigating-catastrophic-climate-change.pdf

11 https://www.investopedia.com/terms/c/compoundinterest.asp

12 https://www.forbes.com/sites/cameronkeng/2014/06/22/employees-that-stay-in-companies-longer-than-2-years-get-paid-50-less/

13 https://www.nbsbenefits.com/what-is-the-difference-between-an-fsa-and-hsa/

14 https://www.nerdwallet.com/blog/insurance/what-is-the-difference-between-term-whole-life-insurance/

15 https://www.today.com/money/how-find-unclaimed-money-your-state-t121115

CHECKLIST

OFFICIAL 365 DAY BOOK COMPANION
CHECKLIST

The Money Resolution
Official 365 Day Book Companion Checklist

Goal: _____

☐ 1 Be transparent with yourself
☐ 2 Review a year of spending
☐ 3 Set your goal(s)
☐ 4 Track your accounts & spending
☐ 5 Link bills to one card
☐ 6 Change your bill due dates
☐ 7 Find old IRAs, consolidate
☐ 8 Document your journey
☐ 9 Find and eliminate your latte factor
☐ 10 Cancel a gym membership
☐ 11 Get a warehouse membership
☐ 12 Slash your cell phone bill
☐ 13 Reduce your Internet/cable bill
☐ 14 Reduce your rent
☐ 15 Find a new bank
☐ 16 Check your balance often
☐ 17 Start an online high-interest account
☐ 18 Get a CD
☐ 19 Build a safety net
☐ 20 Sign up for a free credit report
☐ 21 Have past fees removed
☐ 22 Negotiate your interest rate down
☐ 23 Initiate a "no interest" rollover
☐ 24 Pick a credit card payment strategy
☐ 25 Play the credit card points game
☐ 26 Explore groceries, find cheapest
☐ 27 Plan your meals
☐ 28 BYOL - everyday
☐ 29 Try a meal kit subscription (dinner)
☐ 30 Stop paying for coffee & tea
☐ 31 Commit to cheaper entertainment
☐ 32 Clothes: thrift, tailor, and/or repair
☐ 33 Try new shopping tips and/or hacks
☐ 34 Combine sustainability + frugality

☐ 35 Compound Interest + Rule of 72
☐ 36 Create an Acorns account
☐ 37 Open a Roth IRA
☐ 38 Start your own traditional IRA
☐ 39 Learn about individual stocks
☐ 40 Invest in ETFs and mutual funds
☐ 41 Avoid cryptocurrency
☐ 42 Update your LinkedIn
☐ 43 Ask for a raise
☐ 44 Use bonuses to pay off debt
☐ 45 Up your 401(k) contribution
☐ 46 Fully understand your benefits
☐ 47 Increase you HSA/FSA & invest it
☐ 48 Start a side hustle
☐ 49 Sell items (ex electronics, furniture)
☐ 50 Sell clothes
☐ 51 Flip items from thrifting
☐ 52 Complete paid online surveys
☐ 53 Lower your car insurance
☐ 54 Spring for renters insurance
☐ 55 Get term life insurance
☐ 56 Qualify for insurance discounts
☐ 57 Avoid certain insurance options
☐ 58 Invest in home computing
☐ 59 Invest in your kitchen
☐ 60 Invest in your home
☐ 61 Invest in further education
☐ 62 Invest in a rainy day fund
☐ 63 Invest in your friendships
☐ 64 Take a road trip
☐ 65 Lodge for free
☐ 66 Travel on alternative dates
☐ 67 Use credit card points for expenses
☐ 68 Enjoy credit card perks

☐ 69 Use credit card points for activities
☐ 70 Find cheap/free pet sitters
☐ 71 Avoid pesky international fees
☐ 72 Change the way you gift exchange
☐ 73 Score the best deals
☐ 74 Avoid Cyber Week / Prime Day
☐ 75 Rethink Holiday Decorations
☐ 76 Make your Halloween costume
☐ 77 Read 2+ personal finance book
☐ 78 Subscribe to 3+ podcasts
☐ 79 Frequent 4+ personal finance sites
☐ 80 Use 5+ financial apps regularly
☐ 81 Watch 10 YouTube videos
☐ 82 Delete tempting apps and sites
☐ 83 Claim free cash
☐ 84 Have a spend-free day
☐ 85 Adjust you goals
☐ 86 Explore alternative transportation
☐ 87 Donate your money or time
☐ 88 Be smart with your cash
☐ 89 Return gifts and/or sell gift cards
☐ 90 Add to and clean up your inbox
☐ 91 Assign your beneficiaries
☐ 92 Talk about money
☐ 93 Don't compare yourself to others
☐ 94 Set a plan with your partner
☐ 95 Don't become obsessed
☐ 96 File your taxes early
☐ 97 Don't play the lottery
☐ 98 Avoid lifestyle creep
☐ 99 Visualize your success and write it
☐ 100 Get Started + Celebrate Victories
☐ 101 Pay It Forward
☐ Bonus or Other

Goal #2 (optional): _____ Score _____/101

Made in the USA
Monee, IL
29 August 2020

40185720R00080